MW01037326

Make the Word
Come Alive

Make the Word Come Alive

Lessons from Laity

Mary Alice Mulligan
Ronald J. Allen

CHALICE
PRESS

ST. LOUIS, MISSOURI

© Copyright 2005 by Mary Alice Mulligan and Ronald J. Allen

All rights reserved. For permission to reuse content, please contact Copyright Clearance Center, 222 Rosewood Drive, Danvers, MA 01923, (978) 750-8400, www.copyright.com.

Biblical quotations, unless otherwise noted, are from the *New Revised Standard Version Bible*, copyright 1989, Division of Christian Education of the National Council of the Churches of Christ in the United States of America. Used by permission. All rights reserved.

Cover art: © EyeWire
Cover and interior design: Elizabeth Wright

Visit Chalice Press on the World Wide Web at
www.chalicepress.com

10 9 8 7 6 5 4 3 2 1   05 06 07 08 09

Library of Congress Cataloging–in–Publication Data

Mulligan, Mary Alice, 1952-
   Make the Word come alive : lessons from laity / Mary Alice Mulligan, Ronald J. Allen.
      p. cm.
   Includes bibliographical references.
   ISBN 10: 0-827205-03-1 (pbk. : alk. paper)
   ISBN 13: 978-0-827205-03-1
   1. Preaching–United States–Psychology–Case studies. 2. Listening–Religious aspects–Christianity–Case studies. 3. Laity–United States–Interviews. I. Allen, Ronald J. (Ronald James), 1949- II. Title.
   BV4235.L57M85 2005
   251–dc22
                                                          2005016119

Printed in the United States of America

Contents

Preface

In the first two years of the twenty-first century, a team of researchers interviewed 263 lay people who regularly listen to sermons. The interviews inquired about qualities in preaching that these listeners find engaging, and disengaging. This volume is part of a series of four books that report findings from the interviews.[1] The four books do not simply say the same things four times. Each book is different in that each presents findings from the data from a perspective that reveals different interests and emphases from the others.

The scholars working with the study often say that each volume of the series "slices the data in a different way."

Make the Word Come Alive: Lessons from Laity, slices the data so as to identify elements that are shared by many different interviewees. The twelve chapters of this book lift up twelve qualities that many listeners find appealing in sermons. This book passes along advice from the listeners for helping preachers prepare more engaging sermons.

Believing in Preaching: What Listeners Hear in Sermons (Chalice Press, 2005), by Mary Alice Mulligan, Diane Turner-Sharazz, Dawn Ottoni Wilhelm, and Ronald J. Allen, slices the data by looking at how differently listeners speak about specific aspects of preaching. This book calls attention to various clusters of listener opinion in response to each question posed in the interviews and makes the reader aware of the remarkable diversity of what lay listeners think about preaching. The topics include the purpose of the sermon, the role of the Bible, embodiment, perception of the preacher, controversial or challenging issues, feeling, how the sermon shapes the congregation, God's relationship to preaching, and how listeners respond to the sermon. This volume further helps ministers identify and preach to the pluralism present in the congregation.

Hearing the Sermon: Relationship, Content, Feeling (Chalice Press, 2004), by Ronald J. Allen, identifies three modes through which congregants tend to listen to the sermon. In so doing, the author slices the data with a focus on the ways many people process sermons. The major discovery unfolded in this book is that each hearer tends to take in the sermon through one of these basic modes: perception of the character of the preacher and relationship with the preacher (*ethos*), perception of the ideas of the sermon (*logos*), and/or perception of feelings generated by the sermon (*pathos*). This publication tries to help preachers shape sermons to speak to persons in each setting.

Listening to Listeners: Homiletic Case Studies (Chalice Press, 2004), by John S. McClure, Ronald J. Allen, Dale P. Andrews, L. Susan Bond, Dan P. Moseley, and G. Lee Ramsey Jr., slices the data by looking in detail at six full interviews from the study (five with individuals and one with a small group) and articulates methods that ministers can use for interviewing their own congregations. As the subtitle implies, this book brings a case study approach to preaching. Whereas the other books slice the data by grouping what large numbers of listeners have to say about sermons, this one looks in depth at what a handful of listeners think.

While each book has a different focus, they share the common aim of trying to allow the listeners to speak for themselves regarding characteristics of preaching that engage them.

The study was funded by Lilly Endowment through Christian Theological Seminary, Indianapolis. The project team interviewed in twenty-eight congregations—nine composed mainly of African Americans, sixteen made up primarily of persons of non-Hispanic European origin,[2] and three congregations that are ethnically mixed. The questions, derived from the field of rhetoric, asked people to reflect on how ethos, logos, pathos, and embodiment influence the ways that parishioners process sermons.[3]

Our thanks go to the laypersons and ministers who were interviewed. Many spoke candidly in the interviews, which lasted at least an hour each. Despite assurances that all data would be handled anonymously, several lay interviewees felt a certain vulnerability, but wanted to comment on their perceptions of preaching for the sake of strengthening the gospel witness through that medium. The ministers of the congregations in which we interviewed demonstrated courage and grace by welcoming our questions about how parishioners perceive preaching. We tried to make it clear that the interviews were not a referendum on the preaching of the local pastor, but preachers can also feel vulnerable when laity in the congregation are being asked even general questions about qualities of preaching that they find more and less meaningful.

We appreciate the guidance given to the project by Nancy Eiesland, Professor of Sociology of Religion at Candler School of Theology, Emory University. Where we have departed from her advice (or did not seek it), the project team alone is to blame. We also thank the two project assistants who entered into this work with a great spirit—Owen Cayton and Kara Brinkerhoff Faris. Melissa Green patiently transcribed the interviews from tape recordings. Several leaders of Christian Theological Seminary receive our praise because of their support: Edward L. Wheeler, President, as well as the Deans who served during the conception and carrying out of this project (D. Newell Williams, Clark M. Williamson, and Carolyn R. Higginbotham). We are honored to acknowledge the Religion Division of the Lilly Endowment, who expressed interest in this project far beyond simply funding it, especially Craig Dykstra, Christopher Coble, and Jean Smith.

Introduction

Many preachers silently ask themselves: "What kinds of material in sermons do listeners find more (and less) engaging?" "While maintaining theological integrity, what practical things could I do in preaching to increase the likelihood that parishioners will pay attention to a sermon and take seriously its concerns?" "Are there things I should avoid in preaching?"

The chapters of this work draw from a rich resource that has seldom been explored in a systematic way to guide preachers in responding to such questions. We asked for help from members of congregations who attend worship Sunday after Sunday, listening seriously to what preachers have to say from the pulpit.[1] Because many of these persons consider their faith essential to their lives, they provided wonderful assistance for those of us who are ready to learn how to make our preaching better. These lay listeners are a special type of expert in preaching, for they love God, they love the Bible, and almost all of them love their preachers. The study described in the Preface discovered that, when asked, listeners could often skillfully name qualities that draw them into sermons and qualities that put them off. This book, and the study from which it derives, is one of the first large-scale attempts to report how listeners themselves describe the experience of hearing sermons and to note how those reports can influence preaching. The fresh element in this book is letting the listeners speak for themselves.[2] The information presented comes from a wide variety of persons whose life experiences cover diverse settings over many years of listening to a rich assortment of preachers. What a blessing to the church and to preachers who incorporate these qualities into sermons.

The authors whose names appear on the cover have distilled the material into twelve subject areas, citing characteristics that many listeners say make a sermon inviting. When these qualities are present, people say they are more likely to pay attention than when these attributes are missing. Of course, in the total body of the interviews, respondents list many more than the twelve traits of good preaching highlighted here. Yet, these twelve are the ones voiced most consistently (and with the greatest sense of importance) by the interviewees.

However, we need to qualify this effort. One of the most important discoveries of the study (and of considerable recent literature in the field of preaching) is that people hear and respond to sermons in diverse ways.[3] Indeed, within the same chapter, we cite interviewees who say they are turned off by some of the very qualities of preaching others report here as inviting. We find such diversity in all areas of listening and responding to sermons—from the kinds of theological content and authority that listeners find persuasive to the kind of embodiment that helps listeners focus on the content of the sermon.[4]

The phenomenon of diversity in listener response suggests that one of the most important parts of the preacher's vocation is to determine the particular dynamics that are at work in the culture of the congregation. With this information in hand, preachers can shape sermons that have a good chance to appeal to the different listening patterns that are present in their specific communities. A preacher who listens pastorally to the congregation may find that the major twelve qualities in an engaging sermon are quite different for that congregation than the ones articulated here. Indeed, rather than claim that these twelve characteristics are universally valid, we should more modestly and accurately say that they represent the twenty-eight congregations in the study. Hence, these twelve areas of preaching are less *prescriptions* to be applied to every sermon in every congregation, and are more *prototypes* that a pastor can investigate, test, adapt, or replace in view of local preferences.

Nevertheless, a plurality of listeners say that sermons that consider these qualities have a good chance of drawing them in. We find that significant numbers of different kinds of people respond positively to sermons that attend to these twelve areas. That is women, men, African Americans, persons of non-Hispanic European origin, members from different denominations or movements, people in large and small congregations in widely divergent areas—from throbbing urban neighborhoods to the open country. Whereas the other publications in this series concentrate on bringing *differences* among listeners to the surface, the present book probes *widely shared perspectives*. Many of the topics presented here were not specifically addressed by research questions, but came from open-ended invitations during the interviews to share—with preachers and seminarians— additional thoughts and ideas that would help congregants better engage with sermons.

The reader will notice that we make extensive use of material quoted from interviewees' responses. Although we have made some modest changes to protect the anonymity of respondents, their preachers, and their congregations, we have not modified or corrected grammar except where we felt it necessary to do so to clarify meaning. The elipses in quoted material indicate pauses, not deleted material.

The first chapter asks for theological assistance for individuals and congregations in the sermon to "Help Us Figure Out What God Wants." Chapter 2, "Walk the Walk," notes the importance of the life of the preacher corresponding to the content of the sermon. In the third chapter, congregants direct the preacher to "Speak from Your Own Experience," yet caution that this sharing needs to have proper limits. The crucial content of the fourth chapter instructs the preacher, "Make the Bible Come Alive." Closely related is chapter 5, which asks preachers to "Show How the Gospel Helps Us." Chapter 6 bluntly instructs: "Keep It Short." Similarly, the seventh chapter calls for preachers to "Make It Plain." Chapter 8 invites preachers to "Talk about Everything." Chapter 9 warns: "Don't Oversimplify Complex Issues," adding the important caveat not to treat the congregation members as if they are stupid. The tenth chapter expands this idea to an invitation: "Help Us Get It Right." The eleventh chapter discusses issues of delivery or embodiment including the essential advice, "Talk Loud Enough So We Can Hear." The final chapter, "Don't Forget to Put in Your Teeth," collects additional pieces of advice, which may seem unrelated, but when heard together provide a sense of direction for preachers serious about taking lay advice to heart and mind.

Several ministers with whom we have discussed the idea of shaping sermons to take advantage of these listener preferences have raised an important question. "Are you suggesting that I abandon faithfulness in order to give the congregation what they want to hear?" The answer, of course, is, "Certainly not." Theological integrity should be the backbone of all aspects of ministry (including preaching) as well as the wider life and witness of the church. However, being faithful does not necessarily mean antagonizing the community. A preacher can often manifest theological integrity while saying things in ways the congregation can best engage. Furthermore, as chapter 9 points out, many congregants are willing to have the preacher help them dig deeper into issues of the faith to "get it right," provided the preacher helps them see how such work benefits them and God's world.

To prepare the book, each of us drafted six chapters. We then read and commented on the chapters written by the other. Mary Alice Mulligan prepared the first drafts of chapters 1, 5, 6, 7, 9, and 10. Ronald Allen did the initial work on chapters 2, 3, 4, 8, 11, and 12. The Appendix contains two sermons—one from each author—that show how we have tried to put into practice many of the important things that we have learned through the study.

The themes in this book intertwine with one another across the chapters. Because human communication is such a multifaceted phenomenon, which takes place on multiple levels, it is impossible to maintain strict demarcations between the different topics and chapters. While it is useful to isolate these twelve motifs for discussion, their interaction in an individual and in a congregation is often complex.

As with any initiative in leadership in the church, ministers who adjust their preaching to take account of the ideas in this book will likely want to get feedback from the congregation to ascertain the degree to which the adjustments are actually enhancing communication with the congregation through preaching.[5] Such feedback could be gathered by a minister or priest in several ways. The minister may listen to parishioners in the midst of everyday ministry, or distribute a written response survey in a Sunday bulletin.[6] Someone from outside the congregation could hold a small group interview with congregants,[7] or individuals could be interviewed separately.

With unending appreciation for the candor and good humor of the 263 laity interviewed in this project, we humbly offer their advice, acknowledging that we may have inevitably altered what they said by our own picking and choosing. For any misrepresentations or mistakes in interpretation, we apologize. For any assistance this collection of advice provides to make preaching better, we invite you to thank the laity of your own congregation since the persons represented here remain anonymous.

CHAPTER 1

Help Us Figure Out What God Wants

This is an advice book that shares ideas and opinions from laity in twenty-eight congregations. One of the most interesting and perhaps important discoveries from our research was the deep desire many persons report for sermons to tell more about the Divine. Who is God? How can we know about God? What does God offer our world? What does God want from our lives together and individually? People seem at times almost desperate to hear more about God. In this chapter, while we look specifically at responses about God, we also encourage the reader to keep these ideas as underpinnings for conversations throughout the book.

When researchers asked each interviewee what they want or hope to hear about God in the sermon, one thing became clear immediately. People are not hearing all they want to know about God from the pulpit. Their requests for help to know more about God fall into two loose categories. First, people just want to know who God is, what is God like. Second, they have specific questions about the Divine. We divide these two groups of comments into separate sections below. In the remaining sections of the chapter we look at respondents' serious concern that they do not know what God wants from them. We share their ideas that the Bible is a resource for finding out about God. We look at the belief some people have that God is really beyond our comprehension, and we also look at the role of the preacher in making God known.

First, Help Us Know Who God Is

In asking for direction about knowing who God is, many answers in the interviews reveal an explicit desire to hear sermons about divine mercy or power, as if these characteristics would help one know God best. Those who want to hear about divine grace obviously believe in God's grace, but they appreciate frequent reinforcement that God's forgiveness continues to be extended to all. For instance, a typical response to the question about what one wants to hear about God is: "I think first of all affirming God's presence and then affirming God's goodness. God's mercy and grace is also important to me, so I want to hear that as part of the sermon. God's love, of course, is an umbrella for all of that. I want to know that God loves me. I want to hear that. I guess I want to experience that, too, somehow in worship."

The eagerness for more words of mercy is echoed in other responses. "I want to hear that God forgives us, that divine love is unconditional and that someday I will know God in heaven. That's where we will meet face-to-face." And another example: "I want to feel forgiven when I didn't quite make it or slid backwards, and that I'm still loved, I guess."

Another significant portion of the people in the interviews express the hope to hear about God's power and control over earthly happenings. To have one's belief in divine power reinforced seems to help a number of people know God better. When asked what she or he wants to know most about God, one person is blunt: "God is in control. That could be whether it's a church in mourning, a church in heightened fear, a church that is in good times." When responding to the same question, another person gives a similar answer: "Probably a reinforcement of the fact that God is in charge. God does have control and does affect life today even though we don't have someone right here talking to us like they did in Bible times."

It should be noted that a substantial number of the interviews took place in the wake of the events of September 11, 2001, so human power-lessness and questions of divine control were on many church people's minds. However, it may be helpful to add that very often the desire for reassurance that God is in control was present in interviews held before those events.

Some people are less particular; they express openness to hearing anything and everything about God. "What do I most want to know about God? Well, I suppose the best way…I want to know all I can about God, realizing that I can't know everything. So I'd like to know as much as I can, but you can't measure a limitless God in a finite vessel. So I realize I'll never know all about God, but I'd like to know as much as I can." A person of a different gender and ethnicity, in a different geographic and ecclesial setting, and from a different denomination shares this view. "I don't come in hoping to learn any specific thing. There's so much to learn. I don't think I'll ever learn everything. I just don't know that's humanly possible. So I don't really have any expectation about what I'm going to learn. I'm just excited to learn."

Some Specific Questions

Other respondents mention specific questions they would like to have answered in sermons they listen to each week, such as details about the return of Christ, why people suffer, why certain people die young, or how humanity can influence God's actions on earth. Speaking of a specific tragedy, one person bursts out: "If God is in control of everything, how can that be allowed to happen?" Other persons cite topics they wish the sermons would cover from time to time. "I'd like to get the preacher's ideas on the Second Coming." And another person: "First of all, I want the truth. Then the next thing I want to know about God is how I can be more childlike and Christ-like and still be an adult. I'd like to know that."

What Does God Expect?

Although such interests as wanting to hear about God's love and power and desiring answers to specific questions surface in many of the interviews, a significant number of those who listen to sermons express in one way or another a desire to know what God expects of them. They often include a desire for both knowledge about God and information about how they are to behave in light of that knowledge. Our research reveals a substantial number of respondents who want the preacher to help the congregation figure out how God wants them to function and serve. Some persons bluntly explain the desire to know what God wants as their main reason for listening to the sermon. Others express a desire for the sermon to help them know God better and then to learn what God expects from them. Although the method of the request varies, there is a widespread desire for help in learning what God expects of humanity, especially what God expects of the listening individual who claims to follow Jesus Christ.

In describing the purpose of the sermon, one respondent puts it succinctly: "I hope there would be a greater understanding of God and helping us in our faith and just trying to live a more effective Christian life." The purpose of the sermon, according to this response, is to learn more about God, which also results in knowing better how to live a Christian life. Another person describes this idea in more detail.

> I want to know what God has to say about it. What does the Creator say? People can say anything, but we need to know what God said and does. I think that's what we need to be doing, trying to be more like God or Jesus, in what we do. Like the young people started saying, "What Would Jesus Do?" We need to think about that as adults, too. What would Jesus do? How did he feel? How did he handle this situation? And realize at the same time that we're not perfect. We are sinners, and each day we have to humble ourselves and pray to be better. That's why we need to know,

"How do I get to be better?" "How do I move from one place to the other?" I think that–like–you come, and you hear the sermon, and it inspires you and reinforces you.

When asked what she or he most wants to know about God through the sermon, another respondent expresses a desire not for more information, but for a closer relationship, which would then assist in clarifying how to live properly. "Gosh, I want so much. To bring God closer. To bring me closer to God. To help me understand how to help any way I can. To bring the community together. Help our youth." In about as few words as a person could use, this explanation of what is wanted from the sermon is given: "That God's available and also what is expected by me." Someone of a different gender, different denomination, and quite different setting shares a personal analogy when discussing what is hoped for from the sermon:

> I think I have so much that I need to know about God, because I still see myself as a very small child. I feel I am still fairly young in my growth as a Christian and my maturity as a Christian. There's a lot that I need to learn about God. So what do I want most to know about God? There's a lot that I think I need to know, but basically in that same kind of always learning about God, I need to know more what God wants me to do. What God wants us all to do, but then of course you personally want to know where you're supposed to fit in all of it.

Another of our sermon-listeners indicates that the closer one is to God, the more one will know how to live. This person noted:

> I think that what ultimately a good sermon does is it makes you think about your relationship with God and how you live your life and how you might live your life differently in order to get closer to God and to spiritual and relational kinds of paths. A good sermon will make you think about those things. It might not get you there today, but it will make you think about them.

A few people give specific ideas about what aspects of the divine nature would be most helpful to learn about in sermons. This person, for instance, appreciates sermons that mention both God's compassion and human responsibility: "I like to be reminded that God loves me. That's good to hear. I also want to hear what God has in mind for me. I want to be reminded of my role. I need sometimes to be on the straight and narrow."

Divine mercy and learning how to be more Christ-like are coupled with a need for the Word to include a message of salvation in this response: "Well, when I listen to a sermon, I want to leave knowing more about God, knowing about God's love. This is what the message is to me, to be more like Christ, and the Word helps to make me a Christian person, and about salvation." Another person simply explains the desire to have two questions answered in preaching: "How is God really going to work in my situation? How can I apply that sermon to my life?"

Although many persons interviewed were clear they were not hearing as much as they would like about God in the sermon, they knew what they want to hear. They want to hear sermons that help them know better who God is and from that connection with the Divine, they want the sermon to demonstrate how God wants them to live.

Lessons from the Bible

Many of our respondents find a necessary link between God's message contained in the Bible and the responsibility of the sermon to unwrap what it means. Although we discuss elsewhere how sermons appropriately make application of scripture (especially in chapter 4), we touch the subject lightly here, for knowing God and what God expects of us is learned by many people from sermons that provide lessons from the Bible. A typical response comes from a person who explains: "I want to understand what God says to me or is saying to me. To get some understanding of what is in the lesson and how that relates to my life, I think helps me understand God better and what God expects of us." An even more elaborate answer comes from a quite different setting, from a person who believes God speaks through scripture *and* experiences in the world:

> I probably look for some kind of insight or message as to how these scenarios have played out in the past, because I often believe that God is presenting past messages or stories to help us continue to evolve and prevent past mistakes. I think that God provides us the opportunity to try and learn from each other and learn from the past. I'm probably much more interested in seeing how Christ modeled himself in that situation and how one human can try and model their behavior after another. I think what I look for from God in a sermon or in the world is sort of like God reveals to me through a particular message or word. To me that's often a sort of "Aha" moment. Something connected. Something clicked. And I never know when that's going to happen.

Many persons express appreciation for biblical applications that reveal something about God and about how believers are to live: "I want to know what God expects of me. How can I find out what God's will is for me? Whatever the text is about, how does this apply to me?" The sermon is understood as a key to unpacking the biblical text, explaining important references about God, and then explaining how those lessons apply to the lives of the faithful. "I think the sermon's a vital part of worship. I think it's a reminder of God's word and how we're supposed to be living our lives. I think just to come in and sing praises, or just to come in and pray, etc., isn't enough, especially for new Christians. They need to be fed. I think everyone needs to be fed."

But We Can't Learn Everything about God

A small number of people claim we really cannot know anything for sure about the Infinite and Holy One. They seem to deny either that the sermon can teach anything pertinent about God or that humans are capable of absorbing such knowledge. Our research shows ample evidence that laity's considerations of their faith and thinking about divine power and goodness are not restricted to Sundays. People meditate on issues of their religion day by day. Some of them believe God is beyond comprehension, but that some aspects of the faith can be known. The following response shows the thoughts of a church person in the weeks after September 11, 2001.

> Related to the tragedy of a couple weeks ago, I've heard people and seen on the Internet people questioning, "Why would your God do this?" I think for me to seek to know why God does much of anything is for me to attempt to put myself on the level of God. I think that is just absolutely absurd for me to turn to such an academic introspection of trying to understand God and trying to understand why something was written, rather than simply accepting what has happened and seeking how God can use me to go the next step.

From this perspective, the sermon's job, in part, is to assist in this process of acceptance and seeking God's direction for the next steps.

Another person is even more forthright, admitting that worship attendance is not related to expectations of hearing about God. In line with a good number of listeners, this person believes the sermon provides a time for self-inspection in light of what is learned from how the sermon opens scripture. Instead of expecting to learn information about God alone, the hope is that the meaning of the Bible will be put into words that help the listener understand how God connects with life today.

> I don't know that I necessarily come to hear a sermon about God, because everyday I get up, I'm fascinated with the fact that I laid down and I was asleep. What woke me up? What has me thinking the way that I do? I know that I am created from a being greater than myself. So I don't know that I necessarily come to church to hear about God. I come to hear about how we have this book of God's teaching. So how do we take those teachings and make them applicable to what's going on everyday?

We especially appreciate the candor of one respondent whose ideas of God's greatness and human finitude reveal what the person considers the pretension of expecting to learn anything about the Divine. When asked what she or he most wants to know about God from preaching, our most honest respondent asks: "Who makes up these questions anyway? Know about God? God is that which you can't know anything about really. God is just beyond what you can know. That's why Yahweh [YHWH] had no vowels. You couldn't say the name. The Unnamable. The Unknowable. Right?" When the interviewer pushes on and asks if there is anything the person wants to learn about God from sermons, the monosyllabic answer comes: "No."[1]

Another respondent finds the question unwieldy as well, although not specifically because of considerations of God's infinite incomprehensibility. The person merely states: "That's a pretty broad question. I don't think I can answer that question."

Some persons, however, seem most focused on getting themselves in line with what God expects and do not at first recognize their own expectation to learn anything about God *per se*.

I don't think I hope to find out anything about God. I think I hope to find out...Well, maybe that's not true. I think primarily I'm hoping to be given opportunities to examine parts of myself that maybe are out of whack with what God would like and to be given the opportunity to change those parts of me. I do think that...I'm often kind of knocked back by insights that I get about the nature of life and the nature of God, but I don't think it's what I go looking for, because I don't necessarily think that's terribly important. I think the relationship is important, but I never hope to understand God. I guess I kind of accept it when it comes, but it's not a goal.

This specific concern of learning what needs to be changed in one's life (what is "out of whack" with God's will or preference) is a singular concern expressed by quite a few of the people interviewed.

We now take a brief digression to look at the role of the preacher before concluding the chapter with additional quotations that emphasize the singular desire for sermons to show what God expects believers to do.

Differing Roles of the Preacher

When answering a question about what they want to know about God or talking about becoming better acquainted with the divine, some persons veer off into how the role of the preacher fits into the accomplishment of that task. These ideas range from the belief that the preacher is the divinely chosen mouthpiece for what God has to say to the belief that the preacher is someone who is in the pulpit by human actions and offers important ideas, occasionally some about God. For instance, a few respondents are clear that God has placed a preacher in a particular position to pass along a particular message of what the congregation is supposed to do. "I believe and I hope that there's been a selected person that God has predestined for that moment to share a word. Just like buses need a driver, I think a church needs a preacher." The person continues, "Although there's countless people on that bus that could drive, there's only one designated. I believe that God, through that person, is going to get us to where we need to go." In this view, the particular, chosen preacher is essential for moving the congregation according to God's plan.

From the opposite end of the range, some responses raise a concern about the preacher, submitting a criticism that sermons may highlight the minister to the detriment of the message. "Sometimes I feel like the sermon is more about them than it is about God or trying to be a conduit of God. Usually that doesn't work very well." More toward the middle, but still quite direct, one person believes the preacher's task is to hear a word from God and communicate the meaning to the congregation:

> Address what's going on and what God gives you to minister to the people, but use the word, the Word of God. I've noticed that here in 2001, ministers seem to use a lot of "self." I really believe if you just stick with the word, the word just has enough fire, enough conviction, enough energy, enough love that the people will get what they need right when they need it.

Although such people believe the preacher is necessary, they are not eager to hear more about the preacher than about God.

In chapters 2 and 3, we discuss specific characteristics of preachers and better ways to engage the listeners. However, here we note this range of understandings about the role of the preacher in the pulpit to show the diversity that exists, often within the same congregation. Still, the expectation is almost universal that the preacher will help listeners know what God expects of them.

What Do I Need to Do?

Quite a few persons interviewed made comments indicating they believe the sermon's primary mission is to help them learn more clearly what it is that God expects of them individually and as a congregation. They are looking for direction from God through the sermon. We list several brief responses to the question, "What do you want to hear about God in the sermon?" from different congregational settings (different sizes, different denominations, different towns or cities) and diverse persons (African American and Anglo, representing various ages):

- "Sometimes I'd really like to know what God's plan is for us in all of this, because sometimes I feel like I'm not quite sure what it is I'm supposed to be doing."
- "What God expects of me, I guess. How I can worship God and respond."

- "How I can apply it to my life and how I can be more pleasing to God. What can I do to stay in God's will?"
- "At this stage in my life I want to hear what God wants me to do. Earlier I would say, 'What is God going to do?' But I think you get to a certain point where you realize it's not about you. It's about God."
- "What the Almighty expects. How God expects you to behave and what God expects you to do."

Some of the answers make it clear that listeners often take seriously what is said from the pulpit. Lessons about God and what type of life corresponds best to God's will are what they hope to hear on Sunday morning or Saturday evening. Congregants then think about those ideas for weeks to come, attempting to shape their lives in more faithful ways according to what they have been shown in the sermon. Preachers could benefit from attending to these requests from laity by actually focusing on the content of the sermon, noting how much of the sermon is devoted to helping people learn about God and what God expects from them.

Some persons interviewed candidly share quite specific details about their faith and ways they have matured and hope to continue to grow in the faith. Notice how this person's answer to the question about what one wants to hear about God in the sermon enlarges the idea of taking lessons from numerous Sundays to learn what God expects:

> I don't know if it's most about God. I want to know my purpose, my being, how I live out that purpose and that being. How do I become a better steward of God? I have finally come to a point in my life and I've been so for a few years now, of tithing, but I can tell you when I wasn't. It has been through sermons, through testimonial, through spiritual growth that I have come to accept, understand, and do that. That's been a journey. Sermons help to take people, me, on journeys toward something else. What am I looking for right now? I hope one day to come to church and really know what my true purpose is. What am I really called to do in this church or somewhere in God's ministry? It always used to be for me in this church. I think I've moved past "in this church." I've moved past "in this church" because maybe I'm not supposed to be here anymore. Maybe I'm so hung up in trying to figure out what I'm supposed to do here, I do need to go. Where am I supposed to be? What am I supposed to be doing? What's the legacy that I am supposed to leave here? What am I supposed to really do? I don't know what that is yet. I struggle with that a lot. A lot.

Clearly persons are listening to sermons for help in deciding how to live in accordance to God's will individually. However, persons also understand the messages from the pulpit are directed toward shaping the corporate life of the congregation. Notice this person's desire to have a communal word from the pulpit: "I guess maybe it depends on the day, but I definitely want to hear what God has to say to me and to my church. I guess what I want to know about God is, 'God, what is it *we* need to do differently?' or 'What is it that *we're* doing that pleases you?' Those are things that I like to hear."

When we listen to listeners of sermons, they are asking for assistance from the pulpit in showing how they can live lives that meet God's expectations:

> I want to know about how God would want me to live my life today. How I should walk with God and how I should behave as a Christian and just how I should be living a Christian life and relating to other people with that. That's why I think I like the New Testament and examples of how Jesus lived his life, because we're supposed to live our life like him. So instructions on how you should live your life, the basics, examples, anything like that.

In subsequent chapters, we investigate lay advice on specific topics regarding how to help listeners engage better with the sermon. We have tried to show in this chapter the underlying belief that preaching matters to those who sit in the pews week after week. They are listening with a desire to know God better and to know how they should live according to what God wants of them. In part, their advice for preachers arises from this ever-present desire for the Divine.

CHAPTER 2

Walk the Walk

Many African American congregations–and some congregations of other ethnicities–say that a Christian needs not only to "talk the talk," but to "walk the walk," that is, not only to say the things that are essential to Christian identity but also to live consistently with those affirmations. The same motif recurs in the interviews with both African Americans and Anglos with respect to the preacher–with this twist: if the preacher does not walk the walk (live in ways that are consistent with the gospel), many in the congregation will not pay full attention to the talk (sermon). As one interviewee puts it, "If they don't walk the walk, then nobody's going to listen to them when they talk the talk. Walking the walk is really critical."

This theme is one of the most recurrent in the entire body of data. In this chapter, we not only sample what congregants say about this theme but also list several signs that listeners report as indications that preachers are living with the integrity denoted by the phrase "walking the walk." We note that some listeners say that not "walking the walk" undermines the willingness to pay attention to the sermon, and we comment on the danger that can linger in congregations when trust between preacher and people is lost. We meditate briefly on what listeners say preachers might do to try to restore trust that has been tested or lost.

Walking the Walk Is Fundamental

The following sample of quotations represents only a small fraction of the comments from interviewees from a wide spectrum of congregations. They are African Americans and persons of non-Hispanic European origin; they are men and women from congregations of different sizes, locations, and denominations or movements. They all stress the importance of the preacher walking the walk. A significant majority of listeners insist that the perception that the preacher is not walking the walk undermines their willingness to tune into the sermon.

This sentiment is often stated in positive terms of encouraging the preacher to live with integrity. "I think the 'Practice What You Preach' thing is absolutely critical." When asked to recall a pastor who was also a good preacher, one interviewee immediately said, "That pastor lived what the pastor preached." Another recounts, "You know what our minister is saying from the pulpit is exactly how the minister lives. I don't think anybody in here can dispute that. The way our minister preaches, that's the way the preacher lives it." In the same way, still another listener reports, "What you see is what you get. Our minister is no phony." Ministerial integrity can even issue in an emotional component. "For me, what is touching is witnessing that the preachers really live what they're preaching about."

A parishioner from another setting recalls a pastor who emphasized the importance of visiting members of the congregation in their homes.

> It didn't matter how far they were. The preacher visited every single one. I know this, and I went along to quite a few. This is a good thing—when you see someone not only talking about it but also putting it into practice. When the minister talked about it, it was like, "I know you're telling the truth. This is exactly what you do. And we should be doing it also." Sometimes people say things, and you don't know whether they're just saying it or whether they truly believe it and live it. Our minister lives it. I know that for a fact.

The preacher's life, when statements and behavior confirm one another, is evidence that the congregation can count on the content of the message.

Some strong statements are cast negatively, that is, they make it clear that not living with integrity prompts the listener to lose sight of the message. "I think you'd lose respect for the person," upon discovering a discrepancy between what the preacher says and how the preacher lives, "and if you lose respect for the person, you probably don't listen to what they have to say."

For such people, integrity is evidence of the trustworthiness of the messenger and the message. Comparable comments wind through the interviews. "I think they need to follow the gospel. I don't think they can say something if it's not something they believe and show belief by action." The same resonance comes through another remark by a listener. "I have seen ministers up there preaching from the Bible, but their lifestyle does not match up. The credibility is gone because they sit up there and you think, 'Well, how can that minister preach to me when you know what that person is out here doing in the street?'" A similar response comes from another listener, "For me, the sermons I prefer to skip are those where the words and the life do not match, where the minister is giving a great sermon, but I'm a friend of the minister's children and I know the sermon is just words. The ideas being expressed are not true to the person." Yet one more congregant dramatizes this point when responding to the question of what would happen if the congregation became aware that the preacher says one thing but acts another way. "It would make me suspicious of what the preacher has to say. If the pastor can't believe it and apply it in the pastor's own life, I would wonder."

Character is so important to some listeners that they even pay attention to the poor sermons of preachers whose lives demonstrate integrity and trustworthiness.

> There was a minister almost exactly my age, and for a variety of reasons I admired this person more than any other person my age. In fact, I never admired anybody my age. I never thought of anybody my age as an admirable leader. But in any event, this person was a person of such great character that I listened in spite of the fact that I think that person was a terrible preacher. I listened carefully because of that. I overcame a lot of issues with regard to that.

While this report is intriguing and heartening, we hasten to add that a preacher cannot count on many listeners attending to the sermon simply because they admire the preacher's character. A preacher needs to develop sermons that are themselves engaging.

Some interviewees say that being familiar with the life of the preacher adds a dimension to listening to sermons. "I think knowing the person improves the experience of hearing them preach. Knowing them more intimately makes a difference in how much I get out of what they say." Another hearer makes a more expansive report.

> I know [a particular leader of a social movement] personally. This was a person of great presence. Didn't scream and shout at you all the time but spoke to you and told you things that you needed or wanted to know. I got to know this leader from a distance. This leader was essentially the same kind of person with a very strong presence and was able to project to you interesting details and tell you a good story. You want to go to church because you want to know what such a person has today. Our pastor is in that category, that group of elite people with great presence so that you want to come so you can hear what they have to say.

This leader's actions of social witness are congruent with what the leader says. This, combined with the sense of presence emanating from the leader, leads listeners to experience resonance among the life of the preacher, the content of the message, and themselves. They feel a hunger to hear the messages.

Although we stress that the pastor "walking the walk" is fundamental to many people, we do need to acknowledge that a few folk in our study say that the character of the preacher is of little concern. "I tend to focus more on the content of the sermon," says one, "regardless of the person, not that it's irrelevant." Another adds, "Whether I like the preacher is my last criterion because I think that's not strictly relevant." What counts, for this last listener, is the content of the sermon in and of itself.

Signs that the Preacher Is Walking the Walk

Most of the signals that the preacher is walking the walk derive from people noticing that the preacher lives in the everyday world in ways that are consistent with what the preacher says in the sermon.

Many people report that they take note of the preachers' attitudes and behavior in settings other than worship. For example,

> For both of our pastors, I would say they are very approachable and are living what they preach. I have run into enough people who have seen them other places where the pastors did not know they were being seen and just how they conducted their lives.

Other listeners make similar reports.

> Whether it's in a church setting or whatever I've seen our pastor in, and I've seen the pastor in just about every kind of setting, the pastor lives what the pastor says. I work with the pastor's spouse in a mission project, and the pastor is just as fine and wonderful there as anywhere else. That helps to increase your admiration—when you see somebody and, hey, they're living their faith. Doesn't make any difference whether it's from the pulpit or at a dinner party or wherever, that helps a minister.

A member of the study group who works in a funeral home compares pastors.

> I deal a lot with pastors in my business. I'm in the funeral industry. A lot of them I wouldn't walk in their door on Sunday because of the way they treat you. I don't know if it's just they don't like funeral directors or what, and that's possible. They don't want to think about it. They don't want to talk about it. They don't want to engage in conversation with you other than what you have to do. There are churches I wouldn't go to because it's like listening to a tape recorder. I can stand up there and say the same thing they're saying, and it just doesn't feel like there's a real warmth or presence there that says, "Hey, I truly care about you. I want to hear about you." With our minister, it's give and take.

Another listener makes a statement that ties together the various strands of this discussion.

Often times for me, it's not only in the pulpit that makes a big difference with the minister. It's the little acts. There are actually kinds of living your faith that are very important to me. That transfers to the pulpit as far as my openness to listen. I know they're sinners. I know they're transparent, and I know they love God and they serve others. It's very important to me. I make that connection with pastors because I value that Christ lived what Christ spoke.

The interviewee turns to a biblical notion to express the relationship between the preacher's life and attentiveness to the sermon.

This perspective is reinforced for another auditor who glows about "my favorite pastor who didn't care whether you belong to this church or whatever church. This pastor ministered to you, really cared a lot, deep down cared. You knew there was a genuine love for the community. It was love there, just loved us all. You knew there was a genuine love and concern. It wasn't like a duty or anything." This person believes that the sermon itself is an expression of love and responds with attentiveness.

Some listeners, especially in larger congregations, who do not see the preacher outside ordinary church settings or in the wider social world, make judgments about whether the preacher is walking the walk based on how they perceive the preacher's character via the sermon.

I know enough about the families of our pastors to know what life is like for them. They don't pretend everything is wonderful all the time. It makes them approachable, and it also makes it like, "Okay. The pastor understands." It's one thing to get up there and talk about this nice little marriage. Well, sure, you've got a nice little marriage. Then the pastor tells a few things about blowing it. That really makes a huge difference.

Walking the walk for this listener includes the preacher being honest in the pulpit about the preacher's own struggles.

Clues that the Preacher Is Not Walking the Walk

The congregation picks up most of its clues that the preacher is not walking the walk both by noticing how the preacher lives in situations outside the worship space as well as by what the preacher says in the sermon. The members of congregations who met with interviewers typically say they most often notice contradictions between what ministers say and how ministers live when they see the ministers in settings outside the sanctuary.

When you know something personally about a preacher, and then they make the sermon about showing love, and you know this preacher has spoken ill of pastoral cohorts or has been very unaccepting of certain people or made some statements that you don't particularly agree with, then stands up and preaches a sermon about loving all people and showing God's love to each other, and you know the preacher just doesn't do that, you lose respect and you don't listen because what they say is not what they are.

Another hearer remembers growing up with a pastor in the family.

I think with our minister, what you see is what you get. My grandfather was a pastor, and I was around a lot of pastors, so you can see the different personalities when they were not at church. Sometimes the church personality didn't line up with what was outside the church. Our minister I've seen on social occasions, and everything lines up. That always struck me growing up, that in the church the ministers had to be real pious, but behind closed doors, some of the ministers acted totally differently. Sometimes they were acting the way they were telling everybody not to act when they were in church.

When things do not "line up" between what the preacher tells others to do and what the preacher does, this hearer is troubled, as is someone whose business serves churches.

I feel like I've had an inside look at a lot of churches because I have [worked with congregations as part of my money management business] for a long time, and I've gone into the churches. A lot of times you hear a minister, you hear a message, and then the preacher gets out into the public and is seen there and is speaking about money. That preacher is a totally different person, somebody that you wouldn't trust your kids with. It is apparent to me that it's a show on Sunday. I don't enjoy that. I like somebody who stays the same all the time. I don't want to have to guess. I've seen so many underhanded things done with money in the church. I just want somebody to be real. If they're up there, I want them to be the same as when they're off the little platform they stand in front of us on.

Lack of coherence between what the preacher says and what the preacher does takes away from this listener's willingness to take the sermon with seriousness.

Preachers sometimes leave traces of the fact that they are not living with integrity in the sermon itself. Some listeners call attention to the fact that the preacher can fail to walk the walk by not speaking honestly in the sermon itself, that is, by not saying what the preacher truly believes. "They need to have integrity. They need to say what it is they truly are."

Another congregant makes a parallel point. "They have to be honest. They can't be trying to tell you something they don't believe in. They need to be coming from the heart and from their mind and be honest with what they're talking about."

Along this line, several parishioners respect the preacher who says things in the pulpit that may not be popular.

Whether you want to hear the answer [to a problem with which an individual or congregation is struggling], tough. It's not neat and tidy, because the preacher will probably tell you something different. It might be something you don't want to hear, but the preacher tells you from scripture and shows you. I really appreciate that.

Ministering with integrity can involve "telling you what you need to know, not just what you want to hear." Note the listener's evaluation: "I really appreciate that."

An Unhappy End to a Pastoral Relationship Can Hamper Listening for a Long Time

A pastoral relationship with a parish that comes to an unhappy end can create wariness between some parishioners and subsequent ministers. Indeed, some members will be hesitant, at least initially, to take the sermons of the next pastors with full seriousness, especially if the troubled pastorate involved problems with the preaching, as we hear in this extended and poignant segment of a small group interview.

INTERVIEWER: Can you give an example of a sermon that left you cold?

INTERVIEWEE 1: I heard one. The minister said one time, "Do as I say, not as I do." From that day on, that preacher was not much of a minister to me.

INTERVIEWEE 2: That minister was something.

INTERVIEWEE 3: Lots of people heard that, too, and it was a terrible time at the church.

INTERVIEWER: What was it that was so disturbing about that statement?

INTERVIEWEE 1: Well, number one, the minister was not being true to God and to the faith but was saying and doing things that were totally unchristian. That was just one thing that the minister said out loud in the pulpit. There were also a lot of other things the minister did through the congregation and what the minister said.

INTERVIEWER: I think a comment like that can sort of stay in the life of a congregation.

INTERVIEWEE 2: It's just starting to go away. We had some healing years after that. Some other preachers have come and gone, and I think we're starting to get over it now. You are just apprehensive every time you get a new minister. Are we going to have to go through what we did before?

As the interview proceeds, the members of this small group confirm that they have had difficulty tuning in to the preaching of subsequent pastors.

They become willing to listen more carefully only as they come to perceive the new pastors as trustworthy persons.

To be sure, one failed relationship between pastor and congregation does not completely doom those of the next generation, but it can decrease the congregation's willingness to trust the next pastor, or two, or three, or even more.

Can a Preacher Restore Trust?

A handful of interviewees report on pastors' attempts to restore trust in situations in which the preacher has lost the confidence of the congregation by violating the walk. Thinking about how the pastors in one congregation deal with little flub-ups, especially in the pulpit, one listener reports.

> The preachers can laugh about it. They'll laugh and come back and apologize if they know they have overdone something in the pulpit. If they have misspoken or even were full of themselves in speaking, they will come back and apologize for that, which I appreciate. Even when they're telling stories about themselves–either good or bad–even those can sometimes get carried away. The sermon is not really about them. It's really about God. They will sometimes come back and say, "I talked about myself too much, and I'm sorry."

This attitude usually, as one respondent puts it, "works some repairs."

Of more serious lapses in ministerial attitudes and behavior, a listener suggests an important Christian practice. Thinking about a circumstance in which a minister says one thing and does another, doing damage in the congregation, a listener recommends that the preacher seek forgiveness from the congregation.

> I don't think you necessarily need to explain everything. I don't think everything is all our business, but I think if something happened, say a preacher had an affair, I don't think the preacher needs to stand up and give the details, but could say, "I've done some things that caused harm to people. I'm really sorry." I think that would help. I think the preacher would have to do that.

These hearers do not imply that trust can always be restored through the application of a formula for forgiveness. This is borne out by congregants from another community who tell of a pastor who sought congregational forgiveness after a pastoral indiscretion. This attempt only served to accentuate the pain and brokenness of the situation.

That minister preached a sermon that a congregant remembers as making an important point, and yet was hard for this person to receive because of the pain of the situation in the congregation. As the person recalls, the minister preached:

> Yes, you can be right about something. You can be right from here until doomsday, but just being right isn't enough. Sometimes you have to bend a little bit and see other people's things and not just worry about being right. You have to worry about being human and realize that people make mistakes, even pastors and priests and stuff. That it is not our place to judge. It's not our place to revel in somebody's humiliation. Sometimes you've just got to shut your mouth, be the better person and go on.

The interviewer asked what happened after the sermon. The interviewee responds, "It split. The sermon was something that everybody needed to hear, and it was very thought-provoking and everything. But the church had like three hundred members, where I think now that poor little church has like fifty members. It was a very traumatic thing. Something I hope I never see again."

The respondent concludes that while the theme of the sermon may have been theologically on the mark, the congregation did not perceive the preacher as a trustworthy vehicle of the message. Pastor and congregation need to have a sufficient sense of congregational connection. Then they will both know whether such an effort has a chance of being positively received, whether some other course of action might have a better chance of effecting reconciliation, or whether pastor and parish would be better served by dissolving the pastoral relationship.

An insightful interviewee starkly portrays the stakes for many listeners when the preacher speaks and lives with integrity (or does not do so).

> It's a huge responsibility for that person delivering the message to also walk the walk. That will also cause you not to believe them or to question when you find out that person, who told you all these wonderful ways in which you should lead your life, wasn't doing it. Then you go, "Well, who am I ever going to believe again?"

A part of the preacher's calling is to help the congregation come to an adequate interpretation of the presence and leading of God. If the congregation is reluctant to believe the testimony of the sermon because the preacher is not walking the walk, the community's capacity to discern the divine purposes and to respond faithfully is significantly compromised. Walking the walk helps the congregation believe the talk.

CHAPTER 3

Speak from Your Own Experience

A plethora of people in congregations interviewed in this study indicate that they are engaged by sermons in which preachers refer to their own questions, struggles, insights, and joys. This awareness prompts one listener to advise the preacher to "speak from your own experience."

These listeners are not voyeurs who want to peer in the windows of the pastor's life. They are simply drawn to sermons in which ministers reflect theologically on the meaning of their own experience as a lens through which to help the congregation encounter the gospel. As one person says, "Tell the truth, and use your own personal testimony. You can talk a lot about what's in a book, but nothing is quite as engaging as when you talk about your own struggles and your own personal experiences and how God is working with you."

In this chapter, we discover that interviewees have different perceptions of the preacher's use of personal experience. References from the preacher's own life can illustrate the point of the sermon and help establish identification between preacher and people, stir the people emotionally, and function as an authority for the claims of the sermon. The interviewees specifically suggest that preachers share their own vulnerability with the congregation, seldom make themselves the heroes, or sheroes, of stories, and bring experience into dialogue with other sources of theological insight (such as the Bible). As we have said before in this book, these qualities interrelate. The study does not provide a *carte blanche* for the preacher to bring experience into the pulpit: some interviewees call for limits on the content of the personal material and on its frequency of use. Given this background, preachers can decide whether and how to use personal experience in the sermon based on the degree to which a particular experience may increase the likelihood of helping the congregation interact with the substance of the message.

We need to note as well that a few people say they do not want to hear about the preacher's own life. One interviewee says plainly, "I really don't like ministers to bring their personal lives into a message. You're not going to change that individual by bringing your own personal aspects behind the pulpit. There are too many other things that need to be preached." Preachers who bring their own experience into the sermon need to do so carefully.

Illustrates the Point of the Sermon

At the simplest level, a number of people say they like for the preacher to illustrate the major points of the sermon with material from the pastoral life. One listener confirms of the congregation's preachers, "Every word out of their mouth isn't just walking through the scriptures. They interject contemporary things with that and apply it to their own lives or the lives of people that they see around them. People, therefore, can relate to it." Other congregants concur. "I guess the term today is 'Keep it real.' If you're going to speak about something, if you make application and use something that has maybe happened to you and it goes along with scripture, you can get the message across of what's going on in today's world."

Something that has happened to the preacher likely has happened or could happen to members of the congregation. "And then another thing that [a minister in another congregation in another state] did as we were there–every week the preacher would relate some kind of personal story that tied the biblical message into everyday life. I think everybody can relate to that. They say, 'I know how that is.'"

Some preachers rightly worry that listeners remember stories without remembering the major points of sermons that the stories represent. Occasionally listeners do make remarks such as, "I can't even remember what the topic of the sermon was, but I remember the story." However, we found that quite a few people could connect stories that they remember to the main themes of the sermon, as with this listener.

I don't think the stories are the main thing, but they seem to be the things that help you remember the content of the sermons and the points that were made. I thought that the preacher's sermon today was very interesting with the story about going to the service at the other church [of another denomination], and one of our other pastors talks about that person's youth. They always seem to provide very pertinent contextualization, like things you can relate to that help you link to the message of the gospel or the other lessons of that day.

Helps Establish Identification

A more complicated benefit of preachers making use of their own lives in the sermon is to help establish identification between speaker and listener.[1] The people perceive enough similarities between themselves that they believe the preacher can speak for them. "Be real. Speak from the heart. Let the people know that you've been down the same paths, had the same kinds of crises and the same feelings of inadequacy, that the preacher is one of the congregation." Another person says, "I struggle with things a lot. I think that the sermons oftentimes help me deal with that, because the preacher helps me feel like I am not alone."

As we hear in the following excerpt from an interview, the use of personal experience can help hearers identify with the preacher.

> The preacher was talking about kids going on a trip and how, when the children in that family were very small, "Are we there yet? Are we there yet?" We've done things like that. We've been there. Things like that make it personal. It's not something that someone is telling you, "This is the way it should be." It's, "I know because I've been there and I can share it with you because you're there, too."

As we note below, there are qualifications on what kind of material preachers can use from their personal lives and from the lives of the people in the pastoral household. Nevertheless, when used judiciously such material can enhance the sermon.

Stirs the Congregation Emotionally

The great rhetorician Aristotle, followed by most people who study communication, contends that a public address is often most powerful in its effect when the audience is deeply moved emotionally.[2] Stories from the preacher's own life are among the materials in the sermon that congregations often find emotionally moving.[3] For some listeners, the experience of such emotion is engaging.

> Our pastor one time talked about a brother. I had other ministers who occasionally would talk about their family and relate sometimes tragedies or really close emotional stories. I think that brings it home. You can sense yourself paying a lot more attention to those times than when it's strictly reading from the text. It makes a difference.

Another congregant was asked, "Is there anything in particular that makes a sermon more emotionally moving as you think about your experiences with preaching?" The response is echoed in several other congregations: "Personal stories, stories about 'This happened to me' where you can really relate to emotion. What if I found myself in that circumstance? To me that's the most emotional."

In another interview a small group was asked, "Are there things that really engage you?

INTERVIEWEE 1: Things that engage us? I suppose whatever touches your life emotionally. There are some sermons, I'll be very honest, that have more meaning than others and that affect people in different ways—different people in different ways.

INTERVIEWEE 2: What is good is our preacher always tries to give a personal story. Like the minister tells stories, and we've heard more human stories about that person's life and stuff like that. The minister lives in my neighborhood. We've all grown up together. When you use a personal story, we're all pretty much in the same boat. That touches you.

INTERVIEWEE 1: I guess because the preacher is human.

INTERVIEWEE 2: One of us.

Another respondent in an individual interview answers a similar question, "Sometimes it's a narrative that's very touching about something that the priest experienced or heard about." The respondent continues,

> I really feel the ministers here—they all really do live. When they give these stories, it's because I think their effectiveness is that they do exhibit an experience they've had. You feel inspired by their ability to see in their life how they accomplish a spirituality or Christian devotion or don't accomplish that and seek to improve themselves because of that.

Another auditor sounds a similar note. "Some of the stories, again, it's probably as good to me as anything. Some of the personal stories I hear preachers share and telling about someone else's personal involvement probably moves emotionally and makes me remember things as well as anything."

The preacher's story touches many of these people as they identify with the preacher. The congregation feels some of what the preacher feels.

Functions as an Authority

Different listeners find different sources in the sermon to be authoritative, that is, to convince them to adopt the viewpoint articulated in the sermon. As we note in chapter 4, for most listeners the Bible is the most authoritative datum, with other resources (e.g., tradition after the Bible, evidence from the social sciences and the physical sciences) being less weighty. Many hearers respect the preacher's experience (and the congregation's own experience) as a voice to be taken seriously as they contemplate whether to go with the ideas of the sermon. We hear respect for a variety of sources in the following remark.

I would say that any sermon that points us toward being the church and points us to commune with God would have authority. That could be by using scripture. That could be by using the example of saints. That could be by using books by theologians. That could be from experience.

Even when using experience though, the sermon should "point beyond" the preacher's personal story. The story needs to help the congregation better understand the gospel and their response.

As we are reminded by the next interpretive remark from an interviewee, authority for some folk is sometimes a matter of authenticity more than content.

> I have almost no personal relationship with our pastor. We talk in the hallway for a couple of minutes and that's it. It's usually kind of teasing a little bit. Beyond that I have almost no sense of who this person really is as a person. I still respond positively to this person giving sermons. I think that is partially because I can tell at least this pastor is human. I get the feeling that the struggle is alive. The preacher is not afraid to show that the struggle is very much there.

For such listeners, the preacher's struggle as described in the sermon is itself a reason to take the sermon seriously. As many listeners hear about the preacher's struggles, they identify with those struggles and experience them as kin to their own.

An important correlate is that the preacher does not have to have a personal experience with an idea or situation to speak authoritatively about it. "If you can do research enough to know and speak with authority on the subjects that you have done your homework on, you know. You don't have to know from experience. You don't have to have had AIDS yourself or be a homosexual yourself to know something about AIDS if you do your homework."

Reveal Your Vulnerable Points

Congregants are especially taken by references from the preacher's life that reveal the preacher's vulnerability. Such self-disclosure is often a powerful mode of identification, as we learn from the following account.

> At that point in time the sermon was more of a personal witness up there. What was the preacher's struggle towards faith; the people that had helped? The preacher really connected in that particular time with me emotionally with the sermon and partly because the preacher took a big risk. The preacher took a big risk to stand up there and bare struggles with the rest of the congregation. That helped make the connection.

Comparable concerns come out in the following exchange from a small group.

INTERVIEWEE 1: For me, the pastors I have liked the most are the ones who are willing to put themselves out there.

INTERVIEWEE 2: As a person.

INTERVIEWEE 1: Yes.

INTERVIEWEE 3: They don't depersonalize and to some extent they don't over-intellectualize.

INTERVIEWEE 4: Yes.

INTERVIEWEE 5: A lot of it is, "This happened to me," or, "This happened to my friend." And, "This is how I feel about it." I've had pastors say that they were angry at God–two of them in a row. They were some of the best ones I have ever saw.

INTERVIEWEE 1: They showed a vulnerability.

INTERVIEWEE 3: That's really good–to show their vulnerability.

We hear a similar idea in a compact statement from a member of another church who reflects on "a pinnacle sermon," one that "establishes the best practice."

I think a piece of it is that it has to be a sermon that shows the vulnerability of the minister or the pastor–that shows that they, too, are human, and maybe they can do that through stories. They can do that through things that have happened to them in their past that shows, too, "Yes, we're just like you."

The awareness that the preacher is vulnerable in the same ways as the parishioner creates a bond, a connection that helps this hearer pay attention to the sermon. Listeners identify with the preacher and feel their own vulnerability confirmed in that of the preacher, while also sensing that such vulnerability is "safe" in the grace of God.

The Preacher's Journey as Model

An important role that the preacher's experience can serve for some listeners is to model aspects of the journey of growth in the life of faith. Some listeners indicate that when preachers refer to points of positive growth in the preachers' lives, this illustrates something that the listeners might be able to attain. After commenting on how valuable it is for pastors to share their questions and struggles with the congregation, one interviewee says, "I think it's really important to weave that into the sermon. That's what people can really relate to. That's what happened to them last week, and they're struggling with it. Now here's what you're doing about it because you struggle with that, so the congregation can take it and say, 'Well, maybe I should try some of that.'"

A brief interaction in one of the small groups makes a similar point, while also calling attention to the importance of identification. The following conversation occurred when the group was asked about a recent sermon that the group had found engaging.

INTERVIEWEE 1: I was engaged when the pastor said the part about where, at one time, the pastor did not go to church.

INTERVIEWEE 2: The personal story.

INTERVIEWEE 1: Yes, and you're thinking, "Oh yes. Been there. Done that." I'm sure that other people in the congregation were relating to that. The preacher had been through that, so the preacher could relate to us, how we would feel. That makes it better for me if you've got somebody that's on your own level, and you know that they've lived that life.

INTERVIEWEE 3: They let you know that they live that life. I think that's crucial to any message. "Hey, I'm a sinner here, too. This is what I've done. This is how it can be fixed. This is why God has in place a provision that we can reconcile."

Following the preacher's journey through an issue or an experience helps listeners figure out how to journey through their own issues and experiences. As one person who is a member of a congregation with multiple pastors says, "In all three of them you get a sense that they are striving, not a sense of 'I have arrived.' There may be a chance for you."

However, some auditors voice a caution. When the preacher's own life only shows up in an extremely positive light, some of these folk feel distant from the preacher and the message.

Some Things Do Not Belong in the Pulpit

As well as not portraying themselves as sheroes, or heroes, preachers need to be aware that congregants think that some kinds of material from the preacher's life are not appropriate to the pulpit. This concern comes across in the following interchange.

INTERVIEWEE: The congregation would tell you that we value our preacher's honesty. You value the openness and that the preacher struggles with problems, too. That's not like you have to say, "The old story doesn't tell it all," though. There are limits.

INTERVIEWER: Don't open the confessional.

INTERVIEWEE: Right.

A respondent from another congregation relives a situation in which former ministers had engaged in some ethically inappropriate activities and talked about them in the pulpit.

I think sometimes personal issues of the pastor tear churches apart. I've seen it—pastors either caught with infidelity or something that maybe is not going right in their life. They're undergoing some trials or tribulations or whatever you want to call it. I think sometimes when that type of personal issue starts to become the touchstone of the sermon—if you understand what I'm saying—I think sometimes even if it's heartfelt it can really do some damage. I've seen it happen twice, and it can really do some damage to a congregation when all of a sudden the distance is gone.

This person continues, "I think they thought that, to be honest, they were going to bring their private life and what they were doing into church. It backfired in such a resounding bad way. I had to leave that parish."

A member of another congregation stresses that while a sermon can refer to the experience of the preacher, the sermon needs to focus on God and not on the experience.

The sermon has to be about teaching. I think if it's not, then there's a problem. Because if it's a sort of self-performed self-revelation or something like that, a performance of self, that would be wrong. So when you're telling stories about your childhood, what's the difference between the person who's performing self in a sort of egocentric fashion and the person who's using experience as a way of teaching others?

The interviewee admits, "That's a very delicate line," but urges preachers not to cross it.

After commending a preacher who is "very good at using a variety of stories," a congregant explains,

I know pastors that they always pull from the same experience that they've had or they pull from their family life or from another job they might have had or something like that. Our minister is very good at balancing it from everywhere. This minister gets stories from everywhere. Sometimes they're parables from the Bible. Sometimes they're stories the preacher has read from a book. Sometimes they come from the preacher's life or from someone else's life.

Of the different sources of illustrations, this person says, "That's something I appreciate."

Don't Go to the Well Too Often

In addition, several people in our sampling encourage ministers not to return to personal experience in a deeply self-revelatory way every week. After ruminating about a preacher who told stories from the preacher's own life seemingly every week, a parishioner indicates of another minister, "This [second] minister had a wide range of stories. This minister didn't always use the minister's own life, wasn't always on the spot." To be sure, this listener sometimes connects with the first preacher's experience, but when the sermons contain experiences from a wider array of sources, the listener is not only drawn to the "preacher's spot," but, by identifying with others, "you create your own spot. You draw from it and it applies to you, whereas with the other preacher, sometimes it applies to the preacher but you don't necessarily take it in for yourself." Another congregant says that, particularly with stories from the preacher's life that are deeply emotional, "You have to be careful. You can't go to the well too often."

When considering using anecdotes from the lives of people the congregation knows (especially the preacher's family), a preacher needs to seek their permission for the preacher to refer to them in the sermon. The sermon should not leave them embarrassed. One preacher who does mention people from the congregation by name in messages makes a practice of calling them to get their okay before using their names (or using details that would lead other members of the congregation to recognize them).

At its best, the use of personal experience not only helps the congregation grasp the point of the sermon but also points the congregation to God. Preachers who use personal experience in the sermon need to be disciplined so that the experiences serve the purpose of the sermon.

CHAPTER 4

Make the Bible Come Alive

In describing engaging sermons, the following quote from an interviewee brings together several traits most frequently mentioned in the interviews. "I like preaching that is scripture-based. I like for the preachers to come with a sermon that is scripture-based and one that is clear." Some other interviewees place more emphasis on preaching and community and on the sermon evoking emotion. However, nearly all seek sermons in which the Bible has a central place, that are clear, and that are related to life.

Elsewhere in the book we focus on how listeners perceive clarity and life-relatedness.[1] In this chapter, we explore the most frequent desire that listeners express in regard to the Bible, namely for the preacher to "make it come alive." As we shall see, listeners take the Bible as a significant authority in Christian life. For many congregants, making the Bible come alive includes interpreting the significance of the Bible for today. The listeners in our study articulate approaches for using Bible in the sermon that appeal to many of them. We end with a note for worship leaders as well as preachers: congregants appreciate the expressive reading of the Bible in public worship.

Multiple Views on the Bible as Authority

Although nearly everyone in the study asserted that the Bible is fundamental to the sermon (and to Christian life), when we pay attention to *how* the interviewees talk about the function of the Bible, we find multiple views on the nature of biblical authority in the church. As the writing team of *Believing in Preaching*, another volume in the Channels of Listening series, points out, one of the preacher's responsibilities is to discover the different viewpoints on the Bible and authority at work in the congregation and to dialogue with these viewpoints.[2] For some listeners the Bible is the *single* source of truth. For them, to be acceptable to the church, a viewpoint or doctrine must be found in the Bible. "If you're going to say something, then have the reason for it. Be biblically based. I think we've turned away from that an awful lot. If you take away the Bible, then I get nervous."

Another listener approves of the pastor who approaches the sermon with the Bible with the attitude, "This is what God says, and if you have a problem with it, you're not having a problem with me. You need to talk to God about it." For such listeners, the sermon can simply apply biblical truths directly to today. The preacher needs mainly to help the congregation determine what a biblical text means and then to state its application to the contemporary world.

Many people who believe that the essence of the Bible comes directly from God still recognize that human perceptions differ regarding what the Bible says.

> I believe the Bible is the revealed Word of God, but I also believe that it's not clear in my mind that the translators are following the original script that may have been revealed. We're not sure that the translation is what God meant. I'm willing to accept the fact that there are various ways of interpreting what's written down. The longer I guess on my own personal Christian growth, the more I realize that it may actually be that way by divine intent. It may not be the best analogy, but a lot of people refer to our Constitution as being a very flexible document, [with]our ability to look at it different in the context and current time. I think the Bible is really that way as well if you let it. It has a central message of course. For example, the spouse of somone with whom I work is a minister here at another local congregation [of a different denomination], and my assistant was complaining to me about one of their members who believes that the *King James Version* was the only version of the Bible. I talked to my wife about that. You have to be careful not to think that one translation has all the answers.

This worshiper is not only willing to attend to different possibilities for translating the Bible, but thinks it is important to do so. The analogy with the Constitution suggests that the listener has in mind not only translation in the strict sense but translation as a way of speaking more broadly of interpretation.

Others report that they respect the Bible as an authority, but carefully listening to their remarks reveals that, in fact, they gauge the authority of particular biblical passages by the degree to which the passages are consistent with other norms. For example, when asked when a sermon has authority, a hearer says:

When it's educating me about the Bible. When the sermon is not judgmental. When it's not the hellfire and brimstone. Growing up in another church, I always said I worship a vengeful God, one that was ready to pounce on me the minute I made a mistake. In [the denomination the person attends now] or at least in this congregation, I never hear the preachers condemn people to hell. And I never believed that in the other church. I believed that it was a loving God I should be worshiping. In this church, here especially, that's how I'm presented. I'm presented a loving God who is here to nurture me and care for me and not one that's sitting up in heaven waiting for me to make mistakes to zap me.

For this participant in the study, an interpretation of the Bible must point in the direction of a loving God for the participant to grant it authority.

Another illustrative quote comes from an interviewee who appreciates preaching from the Bible, but still evaluates the Bible itself according to the degree to which it encourages respect for women.

For me in teaching, storytelling and narratives are really critical. They are oftentimes the thing that people really remember or can latch onto. I think stories are potent ways of helping people see things differently, helping people appreciate ideas that they might not get otherwise. To the extent that they're human stories that are somehow, as I mentioned before, brought into a more modern society, I think they are very helpful. Some of the stories where women don't play quite as much of a role in the world are a little troubling to me. So that's one of my main problems with the Bible. There are many stories in the Bible that feature women and that talk about women, but for the most part, it's not a very female-oriented piece of literature. For me, that's been kind of one of the things that's troubling at times. I don't see women very often in a lot of the stories of the scripture, and what not. I think about my girls, and I think about when they learn about the church, they ought to also be hearing about women who are involved in things other than just giving birth to people and that's why they're important. There ought to be some active women who are engaging in issues and doing important things and being role models.

Legitimate authority, implies this listener, involves recognition of the presence and power of women. This norm calls into question interpretations of biblical passages, or passages themselves, that appear to authorize mistreatment of women.

A similar concern comes to expression, sometimes subtly, in other listeners who object to certain interpretations of the Bible and who think that the Bible can be interpreted so as to be acceptable to what they believe about God and life. We hear this concern in the following remark.

> Hopefully, the preachers are trying to enlighten you in the Word and help you understand this whole quest of understanding religion and trying to describe, as best they can, not necessarily the surface things in the Bible, but the underlying meanings of things in the Bible. I don't happen to be a person that thinks that everything in the Bible is literally true, but I think everything in the Bible has a lot of wisdom connected with it, and you have to do a little bit of searching to understand and get a little bit deeper than just the surface words. I think that's part of the minister's job is to help you understand the deeper meanings of some of the things that are stated in the Bible. For me personally, I kind of dislike somebody who stands up there with a Bible and is always pointing to the Bible and saying this is the Word of God, and you have to believe every single word of it. I don't like that. I like somebody who brings a little more of a rational approach toward it and tries to explain the deeper meanings in the Bible, bring some understanding that makes sense to you.

For this listener, it is important for the Bible to "make sense," that is, to conform to what this listener believes is "rational" to believe. This listener, and others, believe that serious interpretation (probing the deeper meanings of the Bible), and not simply repeating the surface meanings of the Bible, can lead to such understandings. Such listeners want the authority of the Bible behind what they believe, and they think they can locate such authority by finding a suitable angle of interpretation.

A small number of participants in our interviews say that the authority of a biblical passage (or sermon) depends upon the degree to which it conforms to what they already believe to be true: "If someone is holding the Bible in their hand and quoting from it, they're not going to have authority unless I like what they're saying."

A similar listener indicates, "You know there are people that believe that everything in the Bible is automatically the Word of God, but I just wonder sometimes if it is, if everything in the Bible is the Word of God. Some things that I don't believe are in the Bible."

Still others regard the Bible as an important source of authority, but one that needs to be brought into dialogue with other sources of authority. For example, a member of one congregation says, "Our church has a three-legged stool. I believe it's scripture, tradition, and reason." Another says the "whole community, grass roots," can help make theological sense. "I take my authority more from what I read in the Bible but also my conversations with other people in my small group, and prayer, things like that." For such listeners, the preacher needs to appeal not only to the Bible but also to wider ranges of experience. The sermon is a conversation toward an adequate understanding of how these various sources help congregations interpret the divine purposes.

Some interviewees, however, observe that the interpretation of the Bible can sometimes work against some of God's purposes. "I'm probably more skeptical than some people here about the Bible because, like anything, it can be taken badly. A lot of the bad stuff that's happened over the last couple hundred years is that people pick and choose their little selections of the Bible." In a similar remark, another interviewee says, "People who have perverse agendas is what has caused the problems we have in the world, not the Bible itself."

Help the Congregation Understand the Bible

Although most interviewees believe the Bible is important to Christian community, many acknowledge difficulty comprehending aspects of it. As one says,

> It's difficult for me to understand what the Bible means just based on my view of life as it is today or in this country. I read the Bible every day, but half the time it's difficult to understand the reading by myself. There's nobody to help you. I like some of that from the sermon.

The preacher needs to help such listeners grasp biblical texts in their ancient contexts.

In fact, placing the text in historical or literary context is important to a great number of interviewees. "If you're to use the Old Testament, you have to explain the whole thing." Another listener says, "But there are some things that are said from the Bible that I have trouble understanding or figuring out that preachers made clear to me."

A small group reports that their preacher asks of the world of a biblical text, "What's going on here?" The preacher "asks that a lot, giving you that historical, contextual, cultural background, and understanding the language as well. That really helps me understand the scripture, because sometimes the English translation in today's world doesn't make much sense." However, "when the preacher puts the Bible in that context, it often does."

Another hearer supports a similar pattern. "If you study the Bible, the key things the preacher makes you understand are who the writer is, what the writer is saying, what the subject matter is, who the writer is writing to, and what the point is." By contrast, another hearer says, "I've seen people quote scripture—pieces of scripture—out of context. I do not give those sermons authority."

As we point out more fully in the next chapter, the preacher's task involves more than simply giving information about the Bible. The sermon needs to "help to make the pages of the Bible come alive in that the Bible is not just print on a page, but it's the story of living, breathing human beings that can be related in some way to me."

Congregations seek not only for the preacher to make the Bible interesting, but also to relate it to the everyday life of the congregation. As one parishioner puts it, "I like for the sermon to go from just, 'Oh, I understand that, and that's where it is in the Bible,' to, 'Okay, that's what that means I need to do in my own life to make sure I'm living this text.'" Indeed, in chapter 8 we report that many listeners would like for the preacher to apply the message to the full range of life issues.

Approaches to Helping the Bible Come Alive

While commenting on making the Bible come alive and relating the message of the sermon to life, several listeners mention things that preachers both can do and can avoid to help the congregation relate positively to the Bible.

Most of the interviewees who talk about the movement from then to now seem to presume that the preacher will talk about the world of the Bible in the first part of the sermon and then indicate implications for the current setting. A listener suggests a different approach. "When people interweave the scripture and the application to everyday life, consistently throughout the sermon, it connects with me pretty good–using everyday examples of how the scriptures apply to our life and not belaboring."

We earlier underlined the importance of the preacher describing the historical setting in which the text came to life in vivid and colorful ways. However, some hearers prefer for the preacher's imagination not to be too fanciful. An interviewee laments a sermon about Jesus casting out demons.

> The preacher decided to create a whole sub-story to this person and explain they had a wife and kids and blah, blah, blah, and the preacher didn't really think the person had demons. Just totally took a little piece that was in the Bible and created something as if they were a sitcom writer or something. To me, that had nothing.

Instead of thinking about the message intended by the preacher, this listener spent the sermon time asking, "What is this? Where did they get that?"

Long-time attendees of worship are often intrigued when the preacher offers a fresh slant on a familiar text. A member of a study congregation reflects on the preachers on the staff of their congregation, "They'll look at some parable and instead of looking at the common explanation of it, they'll say, 'Well, let's look at it from another character in the story.' I hadn't looked at it that way: 'What would it feel like if you were this person instead of the other one?'"

Some listeners like for the preacher to work in depth with one or two texts rather than to jump from passage to passage. "My personal feeling is that the sermon needs to be from one passage. Maybe there was a whole other story, but I don't want the sermon to go from one quote here and one quote from there."

Moreover, several interviewees are put off when the preacher uses the text to get to the preacher's own agenda. "I'd like to see preaching from the text stay with the text, unlike the Reverend who took the text and went everywhere else preaching. Sometimes the text is just a springboard for what follows. Those sermons are not anchored in the text. The text is peripheral a lot of times. It's just the introduction to the subject."

Some people say they like to have a copy of the Bible in their hands during the sermon and to follow the preacher through the passage that is the basis of the sermon and to other passages to which the preacher may refer. "We are encouraged not only to bring our Bibles, but we're encouraged to read it as we listen to the minister."

Other listeners appreciate the preacher giving them handy ways to help remember and use aspects of the sermon. A congregant tells about a sermon that drew three theological lessons out of a biblical text. The worship bulletin contained blank cards that would fit inside a wallet. During the sermon, the minister invited the congregation to write down the three lessons and carry the cards in their billfolds. "It was so practical that everybody could take it home with them." Every time the congregation uses the little cards, "that's an extension of the sermon."

Although quite a few listeners say they want the preacher to explain the Bible and help them relate it to life, many also say they want the preacher to allow them some interpretive space. "I think everybody interprets things different ways. I just like the way this place lets you think on your own. It gives you guidelines, sort of, but it lets you think on your own." A preacher, of course, needs to help the listening community identify boundaries of acceptable interpretations.

Indeed, some listeners from both the liberal and conservative ends of the theological spectrum are disturbed when the preacher uses the Bible to bludgeon the congregation. Asked about the role of the Bible in preaching, a participant in the study replies, "Here is the one thing I think it should not have. Some preachers like to preach with it like a club. They like to wave it and hit it and smack it."

One of our primary roles as authors is to report leading themes in the data, thus we are compelled to report a custom that helps the Bible come alive for many listeners but about which we have reservations: the preacher assuming the role of a biblical character. The following report is typical of people who like the preacher to take on the role of a biblical persona.

> I've had them put on robes, period pieces, and speak through a
> sermon from the point of view of a biblical character, the whole
> sermon. It is very interesting. One did the sack cloth and ashes
> kind of thing from one of the wild Old Testament prophets. That

was wonderful. It was memorable, and I can remember it to this day.

When asked whether such sermons are memorable because they are entertaining, this hearer responds, "No. I think the content was important. You had to look at this from the point of view of the character who was talking or listening to this prophet."

Our reservations are that the sermons we hear in this mode have tended to rely on fanciful reconstruction of the interior feelings of characters from the Bible and to drift into sentimentality and schmaltz. Indeed, some such presentations are hokey. Moreover, listeners may take the preacher's fanciful additions to the biblical passages as having the same authority as scripture itself. Indeed, some in the congregation may not be able to distinguish between where the scriptural element in the sermon ends and the preacher's interpretation begins so that the imaginative elaboration seems to them to be scripture. Pastors who would enter into this mode of preaching need to do their homework very carefully.

Read the Bible Expressively in Public Worship

Several of the people in our sample ask preachers and worship leaders to read the Bible expressively in the service of worship. An interviewee reports a pastor who "has a style of reading scripture that most people react positively to. This preacher has a lot of pauses and emphasis and stuff. Voice inflection." Another listener enumerates traits that mark communicative embodiment. "Clarity. Enunciation. Pronunciation. When reading scripture, slow down. I think we rush through things. I hear pastors and preachers rush through saying 'The Lord's Prayer.' Yadadadada. Wait a minute. That's almost just like routine." This listener wants the scripture reading itself to be "alive." An animated style of reading helps this listener approach the sermon with the conviction that the biblical text is interesting.

In one of the congregations in the study sample, the minister learns the scripture lesson by heart and speaks it with great expression, almost like telling a story. Indeed, this minister often stands in the middle of the worship space to speak the Bible passage—speaking with emphasis, using gestures, and moving around.

> Having it memorized comes off as more free-flowing, and for me it makes it easier for me to listen to. If somebody is reading a scripture, reading verbatim scripture, then if you're not following along in the Bible, then...I don't know where I was going with that. It's easier...I find it easier listening to our minister that you're not distracted. I'm able to listen better than being...For me it's less distracting, I guess, that the preacher stands up there and recites the scripture, more so than reading it. How that affects the sermon,

it just keeps me more attuned from the beginning. For some people, when they hear the scripture, they're already asleep at the scripture before they get to the sermon. They can't hold their attention.

When asked whether this approach to the scripture lesson helped prepare for the sermon, another member of the same congregation affirms, "I think so, because you become more involved with the preacher as a speaker than if the preacher were just standing there. For me at least, it does."

Not surprisingly, some of the laity interviewed for the study read the Bible in public worship from time to time. When one of the interviewees describes how he or she reads scripture in worship, that interviewee is also describing qualities that are appealing when others read the Bible aloud.

When I read scripture, I don't read scripture; I read it as I would a story with voice inflections different for the different people who might be speaking. I think the same can be true in a sermon, not necessarily a dialogue sermon. It could be a single person taking both parts of the dialogue, if you will. That, to me, draws me in.

This congregant concludes, "Monotony in reading the Bible can often be a terrible enemy to a good sermon." Another congregant, who reads the Bible in the service, comments similarly:

I think one of the things that I mentioned was one of the things that distracts me from a great sermon is when the scripture, when read by a lay person, is not delivered very well. Obviously, they've gotten it that morning, hadn't really thought about how they were going to convey it to the rest of the members of the congregation even though it's in print in front of us in our bulletins as well. That can really set a tone for a sermon...As somebody who does that in our church, people come up to me and say, "I really loved how you read the scripture. It really brought it home to me and really helped me better understand it." For people who are auditory learners, that's very critical. But this happens right before our minister steps into the pulpit. If somebody has read their reading, and it's very dry and monotone, the minister doesn't have a very good "opening act."

The twofold importance of understanding the Bible in its own right and of the public reading of the Bible contributing to the mood with which the congregation begins the sermon prompts us to suggest that ministers and worship leaders need to do all that they can to help this part of the service "come alive." Indeed, we think that the preacher should ordinarily read with expression the Bible passage(s) on which the sermon is based. If lay people read the Bible publicly, the congregation should provide training for public reading.

Giving brief background on the historical setting of the passage before beginning the public reading is another practical suggestion from our interviewees. "More often than not, the preacher sets the context of the scripture before reading it. 'This is Paul's message. This is the reason the apostle was writing it.' To me that adds so much more than just standing up there and reciting."

Although we have noticed different ways that people view the Bible and its authority, one theme runs throughout the various clusters of perceptions: many are touched, even transformed by encounters with the Bible. The likelihood that people will be touched by the Bible increases when the text is read expressively in public worship and when the preacher explains the historical context and helps the congregation identify points at which the passage interacts with the world of today. When that happens, listeners repeatedly report incidents such as the following.

> The preacher was teaching us from the Bible, but it was the topic of legalism. I always wanted to justify everything. "These people over here are ninety percent good, so they should be okay. Those people are eighty per cent good; they aren't quite as good." But grace is: "Forget it. Christ gave you grace." Everybody is the same. The preacher was able to explain that very well. It changed me. It took a lot of weight off me. I don't worry about all that legalistic stuff anymore.

Preachers who seek such results will set aside time for the careful study of the Bible and will listen pastorally to the congregation to help identify how encounters with the Bible can help the congregation better interpret the divine leading and purposes.

Show How the Gospel Helps Us

The title of this book, *Make the Word Come Alive*, is a solid reminder that listeners in the pews want to hear a divine word (usually from the Bible) in a way that brings God's message to life. We keep before us the memory of the numerous responses in the interviews of the importance of scripture to those who listen to sermons. Chapter 4 details that importance.

However, it is not only explanation of biblical meanings that is important to sermon listeners. In this chapter, we look more closely at the desire of the laity for the preacher to push beyond mere Bible study. They want sermons to do more than just explain what the texts meant in the ancient world, as important as that task is and as dearly as the listeners want a lively presentation of the meaning of the text. Laity firmly express an additional desire: to show how God's good news of Jesus Christ makes a difference in the world of the twenty-first century. They state time and again in a variety of ways the need for the preacher to "show how the gospel helps us" in our daily lives.

What Does the Bible Say to Today?

For many of our respondents, the first step in showing how the gospel helps is to apply the teachings of the Bible to today. Although ancient ideas are interesting, people want the sermon to relate scripture to their lives. Sometimes the relation is seen as quite direct. If one learns about the Bible, such knowledge is believed to influence and shape the person's life, as indicated in this response: "All I'd say is preach the word out of the Bible. Tell me the word I need to know—the word about the Bible, about Jesus and God, those kinds of things like that. Doctrine. I want to know what's in that Bible. I can't read everything. I want to know as much as I can coming from that way with other believers. That makes me a better Christian."

When the sermon teaches about the Bible, some persons believe there is a direct influence on their lives.

For other people, there is an important additional step. The preacher attempts to explain what a particular passage meant in its original context, but then assists the congregation in understanding how those ideas are relevant to their lives now. The following quotes demonstrate this desire for modern application. After mentioning interest in the historical meaning, one person adds: "How is that pertinent to how we live today? I find that interesting too." Another person agrees: "I think keeping it relevant, keeping it based on sound scriptural doctrine, and giving it in a way that keeps your attention." A person from a quite different setting praises that congregation's minister's ability to show the relevance of scripture for today. "It's a combination in our pastor's preaching of helping today's people with the Holy Gospel."

A long-time Christian offers a more lengthy explanation of how the preacher may understand the congregation's need for what the text meant in context and what it means for today.

> Seems to me the prime opportunity is for that person giving the sermon to try to read him or herself into the more serious aspects, the most important meanings of scripture and relate them to current realities. It's not these stories that happened a long time ago and they're important because Jesus said this or did that, but that they're words lighting our way–lighting our path as we go forward in very troubled times, either personally or collectively, nationally. I suppose in a way to give one a certain amount of courage for the difficult times we live through.

This answer reveals the truth that the life of faith is not easy in our troubled times.

When sermons give scriptural assistance, including words for today, the preacher is showing an awareness of congregational needs. In fact, some listeners stress the importance of making the sermon relevant to the contemporary world and minimize the need for historical scriptural information. The next section investigates such ideas.

Connecting Where Needed in Faith and Life

Rather than listing understanding the Bible as the priority, some persons are firm that sermons are most engaging when they offer assistance for living the life of faith today.

> Relating the sermon to daily life I think would be tops on my list. What two or three points can I carry away from here that are just naturals for me to be able to go out and say, "This is something I can do." This is something that God would have me to do that I

can do to improve my life, to improve my relationship to my neighbor, to my family, to my church, to my community, whatever, I think would be number one on my list. Daily application.

Another person puts it more briefly: "Making whatever they talk about applicable to our lives. That's important to me."

More often listeners express a desire for both Bible study and contemporary application. The following response reveals an appreciation for both, as the speaker discusses the minister's technique of helping the congregation to look at a well-known biblical narrative in a way that offered a new interpretation and application. "It was a story that was familiar, but causing one to think in a new way. Then the way the preacher happened to link that up to experiences in the preacher's life that we encounter every day, how we break out of our normal routine into the real presence of God."

Often the call for modern application grows out of situations in the individual or corporate faith life. That is, when a difficulty arises that people are unsure how to handle, they look to the sermon for assistance. "There are times when something personal is happening in my life, just personal and no one else may be even aware of it, but it's gripping me, and the sermon will just reach out and touch you and you don't know quite why that happens."

A small group interview discusses further why the modern application is so important. "God is giving the preacher what we need to hear. Where else are we going to hear it? How else are we going to know anything to do with issues or whatever in life? We're out there in the world, so this is the one place where I know and probably all of us look for help and guidance. How do we deal? How do we cope?"

In an individual interview, a congregant gives a specific example of a need a sermon might address through scripture and relating the meaning to modern life.

Well, you might be deep in trouble, and you're just at the point where you don't know what to do. I can't really quote an exact scripture, but one that would show you that if you pray about this, go to God about it, you will get some help. God will be with you and see you through this. I think it's important that people know that. They know that God is there to help them and be with them and see them through these bad times. I think they need to know that.

A listener in a very different setting echoes appreciation for sermons that relate to specific needs in modern life. "If they preached a sermon that was particularly apropos for the time or something like that...I've always been rather self-conscious about what I say to a minister about a sermon, but if there is one and they have preached particularly to an event going on, I usually will tell them that they really reached me or something like that."

A final appreciation about sermons connecting to corporate or individual needs in today's world is expressed by some who are eager to have their faith stretched and fed for growth. "I like to feel good coming out of worship. I also like to feel squirmy, a little inadequate. There's something in your life to work on. You're not perfect." And from a different setting and denomination: "I hope that my thoughts and beliefs will be challenged. If I can't defend what I believe, then I might be wrong. I hope I will be fed with new insights, new ways of looking at things, and in the end I'll have a clearer understanding of God's will and what it is I believe, I feel."

What Is Not Helpful?

A few respondents share ideas of ways a preacher may attempt to communicate the gospel that are not so helpful. Quite a few persons go so far as to say that sermons that are Bible study alone are not helpful. This response reveals the reasoning:

> I don't think sermons that tend to just preach by expounding on the gospel or on a passage of the Bible are effective if they're not connected to everyday life. One of the best ways to do that is: "This is the message. Here's a story to illustrate that about Crystal or about me or whatever." People can then relate to that and that helps them feel more connected intellectually. It makes it more personal for them.

In another setting altogether, this response strikes the same tone: "I don't get much out of sermons that stay in the first century. They can talk about works and parables of Jesus. They can pull that in, but I begin to connect much more easily when they use illustrations of people like I am, like contemporary people, rather than trying to pull everything out of the Bible."

Another sermon technique that comes under criticism is described by various terms, but often it is portrayed as the technique of basing the sermon on fear. As we detail further in chapter 11, some respondents find the volume and gesticulation of certain sermons about judgment off-putting, but for our purposes in this chapter, the responses we are interested in are those related to the content of the sermon.

One response articulates that such fear-based sermons are not helpful to developing the faith. "Hellfire and brimstone—some that I have heard that were very frightening. Yes. And really invoked an image of hell. I never could relate well to those and found them useless. I couldn't figure out what I was supposed to do with them." Another response bears a similar idea in articulating when a sermon has authority. "When it's not judgmental. When it's not the hellfire and brimstone." Basing the sermon on fear is not helpful for these persons in finding ways for the gospel to be meaningful today.

Sharing Some Specifics

In this section, we reproduce some responses that give specifics of sermons that show how the gospel is especially meaningful in particular moments of contemporary life. We are purposely allowing this section to be longer, because the quotations contain examples from distinct sermons showing how the preacher has given meaningful application of the gospel for living the faith in our world. It may be interesting to note the detail of some of these reports.

Many interviewees claim at first not to be able to remember specifics from sermons, yet as these examples make clear, when sermons meet persons where they live today, the listeners are touched deeply and are able to remember and recall.

These first responses are perfect examples of what we mean. In a small group interview, someone mentions the desire for more in-depth and practical help from sermons, using the example from a recent family conversation about the need for preaching about relationships. "Everybody tells you to get married, but nobody tells you how to stay married." One of the other participants adds an example of something else that could be preached on to help families where they are: "As parents, how to go to the Bible and study and give our kids and teach them and bring them along."

A short time later, the first participant continues the conversation about sermons connecting where the needs are: "Anything to deal with life issues. Everybody hears that God loves you and all that and that's good, but the real, real things that people are dealing with, again like that marriage situation, is what we need to hear as a people." Another listener of a different ethnicity, from a congregation of a different denomination and quite different setting, also believes that the best sermons address people where they are today. This respondent is able to remember a sermon that connects to a situation in modern life. "I remember one sermon that talked about the woman at the well and I think it's in the Greek Orthodox Church that this woman became a saint. I remember that sermon. I just told our preacher afterwards, it felt like it dug a whole layer of dirt off of women in the church. It really was a powerful, powerful sermon."

A teenager reports a time when a message touched right where people that age live. In answer to a request for an example of what the interviewee means by a "wow" sermon: "Reverend did a sermon on peer pressure, about how people can sway you to do things. It's like you want to say, 'No,' but you don't want to be like, 'Oh, you're lame!' So it was right on key that the preacher was talking about how you can get away from that even happening without lying.

In another small group setting, someone repeats a personal illustration that had been used in a recent sermon. One of their ministers is part time and works another job that includes making client home visits to places of questionable safety. The respondent recites the illustration: "Our associate pastor went into this horrible sort of crack house, and in one of these rooms there was a picture of Jesus. The first reaction was, 'How do these people have Jesus' picture?' Then came the realization." The respondent pauses to make sure that the interviewer gets the realization that God is for all people. God does not belong to us.

"That's the way our associate told it. It was a way of making the lesson clear. I'll never forget that." Another person in the small group responds: "That was vivid for me, too."

Listeners are often quite able to say what they wish sermons would do to make the gospel meaningful to life today. Unfortunately, they do not always receive it. Consider this lengthy response, where the person knows what would be helpful.

> I would always enjoy something that relates it to contemporary life or my life. That will always be what engages me in this process. When we have water cooler conversations at work about, "Wasn't that horrible that a mom drove into a tree the other night and killed herself? And those two kids? What's going to happen to those two kids?" That's not my life, but it's still what I heard last night on TV and what I struggle with. How did God let that happen? What can we do to support moms so that they don't get so distraught that they traumatize kids or drive into a tree? Those are things that we do struggle with in daily life. Or how 168 families put their lives together after an Oklahoma City bombing? I think with the recognition that there's cause of some spiritual pain as human beings and to help us deal with and get beyond that. And also to celebrate when we see Olympic athletes who do very well and who were good to their moms and praised God when they got their medal. The things that we see in everyday life that we should be able to either cope with, deal with, understand, or celebrate, I think, are generally the things that will make you engage most in the sermon.

Some persons tell of specific times in their lives when a situation had them stumped and a sermon made a connection that turned everything around. There are times when the preacher seems to speak a message directly from God to address a question of an individual in the congregation. These sermons that come at key moments in lives of individuals or congregations are obviously remembered, and people relate them with ease.

For instance, one person discusses the importance of sermons relating to life. "I have some serious illness problems. I used to think, 'Why am I sick? Why have I had all these surgeries? What is it about me that this has happened to me?' A sort of self-pitying thing, something that's easy to get into. Then in the sermon you hear of other people, other things that are much worse off than you are. It makes you appreciate your life."

At times sermons can touch a situation that the entire congregation is experiencing. This person reports on a difficult time the congregation is having with numbers and participation.

> That's why I say that we at this church need encouragement during the times we are having. Even when things glorious and grand show up, we still need that encouragement. We are that church that has diversity with old groups, young groups. We have some kids. We have a few, but it's based upon the participation. I felt that we at this church need the encouraging factor to encourage you to want to participate. That comes through the sermon.

The listener expects the sermon to be an encouragement to the entire congregation at a time when discouragement is afoot.

There are other times when people are not feeling particularly troubled by a current situation or unanswered question, but the sermon touches them in a surprising way. Reporting on an All Saint's Day sermon that stirred up emotions, a respondent says:

> There's a boy I grew up with. We grew up in the same town. We went to the university together. We both went off to the army together. He was killed in France. I came back. It could have been me rather than him. I found an identity with him then that I simply hadn't felt before. It was the sermon in part. The sermon set the context. It gave the enveloping structure for the whole evening's liturgical experience.

Without warning, without entering the service remembering this young man dead for more than fifty years, the listener is confronted with an unsettling memory that the sermon helps to settle. The content of the message applies to some unfinished "faith business" of a half century before. The sermon does not connect with an important issue of today, in this case, but of a long-ago issue that still affects one's faith. Knowing such events can occur, preachers will want to consider ways their preaching is answering and dealing with issues people need to know about, helping listeners discover vital connections between life today and the text/doctrine/ or ethical principle that is at the center of the sermon.

In addition to recognizing the phenomenon of sermons stirring old concerns, preachers need to be aware that sermons can also work in other directions. That is, a sermon can deal with an issue so powerfully that it affects the listeners' thinking on a topic well into the future. An older respondent reported the power of a single sermon to last for a number of decades. After reciting who the preacher was, the denomination of the congregation, and the city, the respondent tells of a sermon heard a good many years before. "I remember the preacher talked about water. I forget exactly, but, 'In the beginning there was water.' I think of this now when there is a baptism. The water, parting at the banks of Jordan, taking the people through. The water was present at the creation. I forget it all, but the use of water was very effective." In this instance, a powerful sermon about water, heard years before, is recalled now at each baptism. When the sermon is given, although it is much appreciated, the listener is not able to predict that it will be recalled at every baptism for years to come and enrich those worship experiences significantly.

The reports of specific sermons that address issues of current concern, former questions, and even future worship experiences underline the fact that sermons make continuing contributions to the lives of individuals and congregations. Preachers help these contributions become even more important by connecting the content of the sermon to people's daily life.

Additional Advice for Showing How the Gospel Helps

Some listeners are particularly careful to spell out their advice for preachers. For instance, one member reminds preachers of the importance of continuing to learn and be aware of the congregational context as aids to making sermons meaningful. "I think it is important for our preachers to be aware of what's going on in the world, of what's happening among the members of their congregation. That doesn't mean they have to be there every minute of the day. To do what they can to keep on educating themselves, because once you're out of seminary, you're really just beginning." Another person praises the congregation's priest for preaching in a way that is helpful, citing what the priest does as advice for others. "Our preacher brings optimism. This is a person who actually thinks that what is said from the pulpit is going to affect us, that the congregation will move and change and become more welcoming or whatever it is our priest is advocating. The preacher is optimistic about that."

Preachers would do well to be alert to the variety of questions and issues that are important to their congregation. Some of these topics will be unique to the particular circumstances of their groups; others will be universal, such as subjects of baptism, human need, sin, salvation, and death. In keeping attentive to the concerns of the congregation, the preacher can decide when, whether, and how to address a range of these issues in preaching to the congregation.

A final piece of advice is given in some detail, reminding preachers that the congregation is made up of a diverse assortment of persons, each of whom is looking for guidance in making the gospel meaningful to the life of faith today.

> Be applicable to what's in the Bible, which I'm sure all ministers do, but be able to apply them to what's happening now. Be able to master applying them to all levels, and that includes the youth. You've got to be able to talk to the youth at a level that they're willing to listen to you. You've got to be able to talk to those individuals in their early fifties, as well as be able to communicate with the older parishioners also. You've got to master that. If you haven't done it, then realize that's something that you need to brush up on. You just can't cater to those individuals that you may consider to be the more financially affluent people. You've got to look at what everybody has to offer and be able to communicate with them so that they feel comfortable.

It may be important for preachers to remind themselves that the members of their congregations are sitting in pews week after week hoping to hear guidance for the life of faith today. People are asking for help in making contemporary sense of the gospel, because they believe that faith in the will of God and in the compassion of Jesus Christ means something for their twenty-first–century lives. They trust their preachers to share how the gospel helps them as they face the world each day.

CHAPTER 6

Keep It Short

Ironically, one significant piece of advice we offer from the 263 laypersons that spoke with us is to keep the sermon short. Of course, short is a relative term. One of us has an Episcopal sister who claims, "If a person can't say what they need to say in ten minutes, obviously they haven't thought it through well enough." On the other hand, one of our spouses claims, "It takes ten minutes to get warmed up." Obviously, "short" has no specific time frame.

Still, we want preachers to hear us clearly. We were told, in setting after setting, short is better. Frequently connected with this appeal for brevity was a preference for clarity and a definite sense of the necessity of helpful content. However, we have decided to separate these ideas into their own chapters in order not to lose the importance of each one. Even if persons are clear and helpful, their sermons will be less well received if they are not succinct. It is appropriate to take a chapter to let the laity explain what they mean when they advise preachers to "keep it short."

Our first clue that the length of the sermon was going to be an important consideration throughout the interviews came very early in our research process. During the training of our researchers, we asked a "pilot group" to allow those who would be leading the actual interviews to eavesdrop on their interview conversation as a test case. Our consultant directed the small group as a fishbowl, with the practice interviewer in the center and the researchers-in-training surrounding the "pilot group." During the debriefing of the researchers, one after another expressed surprise at the answers when we asked for advice to preachers. In the small group interview with half a dozen women from a long established African American congregation, each one mentioned brevity. It was not just that one person mentioned the importance of keeping the sermon short and the others nodded. Each added a comment about the importance of "keeping it short."

This pilot small group was not actually part of the formal study. It was "practice," but the authors each remember the group's responses and our surprise at them. If this group of mature, loyal, African American women, after expressing time and again a high appreciation for preaching, one after the other also expressed the opinion that the sermon needs to be succinct, then we needed to be prepared for hearing that directive from others.

A Pervasive Theme

In actuality, we heard comments about sermon length from almost every congregation in which we held interviews. This is particularly noteworthy because we did not even ask a question that directly addressed timing for the sermon. Often the interviewed person turns the conversation to sermon length when the open-ended final question is asked, "Do you have a final word or two of advice for your preacher, other preachers, or seminarians?" "What would you want to tell a preacher that would help her or him engage the congregation better in preaching?"

The advice about keeping the sermon short is often just a brief statement. These examples come from persons of different ethnicities, different genders, different denominations, with more than fifty years separating the youngest from the most senior.

"Don't just be filling up time."

"Don't talk too long."

And one, when asked for a final piece of advice, suggests preachers "not drag things on."

A member of the small group interview of a congregation has a little longer comment, but the point is the same: "It also helps that it's going to be short. The preacher's not going to go on for twenty-five or thirty minutes. Ours is very brief. Some people can't hang on for much longer than that."

Other respondents agree that keeping it short is crucial, some adding that attention spans have their limits. "But no long sermons for me. Could be I feel this way because there are younger...We have a lot of younger people in our congregation, and I think the words that you use sparingly may reach more than a long, long sermon."

Why Keep It Short?

In addition to the blunt comments to keep it short or suggestions that attention spans may not be able to take much more than a brief sermon, quite a few respondents give a particular reason for wanting sermons to be short. Many of these answers indicate they believe the minister is in an agreement with the congregation that the worship service begins and ends at a particular time. This requires the sermon to be a certain length (a length that shortens on Sundays other events are taking place). The beginning and concluding time are understood as matters of mutual trust.

The following two comments are representative. One comes from one of the larger, and the other from one of the smaller, congregations in which interviews took place:

> Stay with the time frames. Sometimes, and I don't blame our preachers for this, but people just lag so much out in the hall, like when there's not Sunday school, and they are socializing, but church was supposed to start twenty minutes ago. So get in here and sit down. I know they will go on in and start the service and leave a lot of people lagging back here. Eventually they get in, but it's like half of the church sometimes is still back here or coming in from their cars or something after the message starts, and I don't like that. I also like to tell them if I know church is over at twelve, and then it's going to be over. I'm annoyed if somebody gets up and goes on for a half-hour, and that's happened before. It isn't always the preacher who does that. I just think you start and stop when you're supposed to.

And from the other congregation: "I do think that holding the sermon to a certain period of time and the entire service to a certain period of time is definitely a plus, and we haven't had that problem here. We get out on time and everything."

Not Everyone Cares about Time

Not every statement about length encourages keeping it short. A few listeners express appreciation for sermons that delve into subjects that matter to the faith, without worrying about cutting things short. They want the minister to communicate a teaching or a message without feeling the pressure of finishing quickly. For instance, this comment from a member of a small group responds to another person's advice for keeping it short. "Actually, I was going to say I enjoy knowing that it's going to be a longer sermon than the quickies that I was used to growing up." In this particular congregation, the typical sermon is about twenty minutes, which this respondent prefers to the shorter sermons of the childhood church. Apparently the belief is that more can be communicated about the faith in a longer sermon, and that makes it worth the extra time. We note, however, that the respondents in the small group seem aware of the typical length of a sermon in this congregation, which apparently does not fluctuate much.

Other listeners in various settings argue that length, especially if the concern is about getting out at an agreed on time, is not an appropriate consideration. The message is the important element, not the time. So flexibility in sermon length makes sense, either longer or shorter, depending on what the topic deserves. "Don't be afraid to wrap up the sermon in twenty-five minutes if that's what the clock says. I see that happen too many times. The congregation will notice. Like the one church I mentioned…It said, 'From this time to this time, we're going to do this.' Boy, it didn't go over two minutes. Don't be afraid to let that sermon go on." One final response summarizes this feeling: "I never wish that a sermon would end. I never do."

Length and Content

Many listeners who make comments about length seem to connect that concern to a significant degree with content. Sermons are expected to have a life, a natural growth and flow, which includes a natural stopping place. We remember the homiletics[1] professor at a denominational seminary commenting about a visiting preacher's sermon in chapel, "There were several excellent stopping places in the sermon. I wish the preacher had used one of them."

Other lay people whom we interviewed share the belief that the good preacher feels the flow of the sermon and attends to the natural stopping point. "Something else I've noticed at times when a good couple of sermons that I've heard in which there was an opportunity to stop, but it didn't stop. It kept on going. 'Wait a minute. You had me. You had me.' A couple more movements like that, you're going, 'Stop! Enough!'" In such comments, one can feel the frustration of the listener. The sermon is over, yet the preacher continues talking. The frustration often borders on a sense of insult that the preacher does not know when to stop or is disregarding the congregation. Persons in quite different settings express similar ideas. This one, for instance, comes from an interview in a significantly different-sized town in a different denomination.

> Make it relevant to your congregation and to the people in the congregation. I guess make your point and move on. Don't belabor. I've heard that more than once where one time would have been adequate. Tell me the same thing in a different way four or five times doesn't make a lot of sense. I've heard a lot of sermons that could have been half as long, because there wasn't really any new information.

Length and Preparation

In some of the interviews, both individual and small group, comments were made connecting a sermonic disregard for the appropriate ending place with lack of proper preparation. That is, knowing when to stop is linked with knowing what actually needs to be said about a particular passage from the Bible or a particular topic.

The respondents seem to be saying, "If the preacher were fully prepared, she or he would be confident about the content, competent in explaining ideas, present a logical progression, build to a conclusion or presentation peak, and then draw the material to an appropriate and timely closing." If the preacher drifts off the subject or wanders around the topical terrain too much, the sermon inevitably falls prey to the criticism of being "too long." Even if the actual minutes of the sermon equal what is typical, the lack of preparation allows the preacher to stumble or ramble.

Many congregants have done public speaking in some setting, so they are aware of the agonizing process of preparing a public address that is clear and succinct.

Note this listener's calling for preparation that includes revising and editing material to make it tight:

> When I write speeches and presentations, I start out with something forever long, it seems like. Then I just start chopping to get down to what I really want to say and the best way to say it, because it holds your audience's attention far longer. I think those are some of the things that would be helpful to a lot of ministers. You don't have to fill the time span. Say a few things that are important.

Another respondent echoes the need for proper preparation:

> We've had pastors who took forever and two days to get to the point in their sermon. They just don't always get to the point. Some people seem like they never get to a point. So I think you need to be focused, and since I speak from that pulpit from time to time myself, I am very much aware of that. We need a point. I have to be careful myself when I'm speaking. To make our point clearly as we can and don't take all day to do it, because I think you lose people. After about thirty minutes, you lose people. I think just be more conscious of our point and get to that point: the main idea in the lesson, in the sermon.

A final example of the relationship between brevity and proper preparation comes from a listener in yet another denomination and a significantly different-sized congregation. "I think to recognize that less is sometimes better than more. Once you've made your point, move on. That having discipline about how you put that sermon together is very important. You ought to figure out for your style, what the rules are and try to make your sermon each time fit within those rules."

Some listeners concur that keeping it brief is important, yet they admit their attention can be held for longer periods when the preparation has been sufficient and the topic warrants extra time. One respondent is a perfect example. This person first claims shorter is better and then also admits length is appropriately flexible:

> I don't think that you have to be longwinded. The hardest thing to do is write a short sermon, a meaningful short sermon. The hardest thing in business is to write a short presentation or a short speech

and say what you want to say. It's a lot easier to use more words than it is to use less words. If you can capture what you want to say in as few words as possible rather than feeling like you have to fill a time span, and you need to deliver it succinctly and simplistically. And then say very concisely what your message is and deliver it with enthusiasm. Passion and enthusiasm. Let that show through. People complain about that in sermons all the time. I don't care how long it is as long as it says something meaningful to me.

Another listener is even blunter. "What makes a sermon too long is if it gets too far away from me personally and you lose my interest." The presentation of the material must not only show proper preparation, it also requires knowledge of the congregants' interests and personal concerns.

What about Stories?

One particular place we notice some people's reporting a tendency of preachers to go on too long is in telling stories. Preachers apparently feel comfortable telling a good tale; and response to a meaningful illustration is frequently positive, as is evidenced by comments to the minister or priest at the door after worship. Because stories go over so well, preachers may tell them with greater detail than is needed for the purpose of the sermon.

One person's comments demonstrate the concern. After praising the minister's tremendous ability to communicate gospel ideas through stories, this listener quietly admits, the preacher "spends a bit more time than is necessary or desirable in giving the details about a story." The respondent was able to report stories and sermon ideas in answer to various questions, so we are convinced the minister is a fine preacher and storyteller, but the extended stories sometimes detract from the power or purpose of the sermon.

We suspect that stories can become overly long because preachers do not feel the need to write them out word for word. Instead, they trust their ability to tell the story, adding details if it is going well and the congregation seems to enjoy it. Illustrations the preacher offers from memory allow extended periods of eye contact with individuals in the congregation. Over and over our research confirms that eye contact is a crucial ingredient of good delivery. Yet too many details or a story that goes on too long for the purpose of the sermon can be troublesome.

We believe this concern backs up what at least one homiletician has asserted for some time. David Buttrick writes that although people enjoy extended illustrations, they "may be much less effective than we suppose."[2] People get caught up into the "world" of the story and "participate emotionally in its pathos…[But then] people will find it almost impossible to disengage from the illustration and to grasp the understanding, which, *supposedly*, the illustration supports."[3] Our research reveals that some listeners can become so involved in the life of the story, they detach from the flow and purpose of the sermon itself. They may remember the story, but not how it served the sermon or explained a Bible passage.

Tips from Laity

Keeping it short involves actually condensing the number of sentences or minutes that one preaches. It also means maintaining the sermon focus, sensing a natural progression and conclusion, limiting details in stories to those that serve the purpose, and making sure the time frame is honored. All these suggestions have some relationship to the preacher's preparation, which listeners notice. "Don't fall into patterns of rambling and giving a long, drawn out explanation when a short, concise explanation would be better." This same respondent continues by giving a helpful analogy.

> Think of going to a track meet and watching the sprints. Watching someone run two miles around the track really bores me after a little bit. Watching a hundred meter dash or a race of shorter distance, it's over. It's exciting. It's enjoyable, and I'd like to see another one. I have sat in sermons where thirty minutes, you get the points. This is over. I really wished it were a little longer. I enjoyed it that much. I walked out feeling better about those than I had the same thing said three different ways for an hour.

Obviously, the definition of a short sermon varies from listener to listener and from congregation to congregation. So what might preachers do to figure out whether the appeal to "keep it short" is being spoken (or thought) within their own congregations? The advice we hear in setting after setting is to make sure the sermons are not just brief, but rather concise and/or precise (note how these words share the root word, *caedere*, meaning "to cut"). That is, laity ask for sermons that say important things about God, the Bible, and the faith with precision. No unnecessary parts. "Show us you are prepared" by keeping the focus, which results in a sermon that stops when it is over.

Often preachers are even aware on some level that their sermons are not "keeping it short." For instance, in interviews with the clergy, we discuss what one might want to learn from the congregation about one's preaching. A minister made the following admission: "The length. We kind of have a little joke here, but I understand that under the joke there's a little bit of sincerity there, that I preach too long. It usually averages around twenty minutes, and I try to bring it down to fifteen minutes and usually end up going over." The minister goes on to say, "I don't want to lose people over that. I really try to approach things like that. We joke about them, and I hear them; and they know that, but we're able to joke about it a little bit."

Surely there are issues more significant about preaching than keeping it short. None of us would prefer a short sermon with bad theology, disrespect for scripture, disregard for the congregation's needs and interests, and no sense of mission or justice. Such a sermon would certainly be worse, but often a simple thing like exceeding the appointed ending time week after week can derail a congregation's attention to the important information and spiritual guidance in the sermon. When listeners are bold enough even to drop a hint (even a joking hint), then the preacher needs to pay attention. If the topic is broached, preachers need to ask themselves whether they are willing to consider taking corrective assistance from the congregation.

It takes additional work to tighten or condense a sermon, and preachers' time seems always at a premium. But most of our interviewees agree preaching is one of the most important things the pastor does each week. So attending to the listeners' suggestion to shorten the sermon may mean more time on the sermon, but important time for the well-being of the congregation and individual listeners.

We also wonder about clergy who would disregard the advice and assistance of the lay listeners. If such assistance is disregarded, perhaps preachers need to ask themselves why the congregation would then be expected to take corrective assistance from the minister. Is the priesthood of all believers not something to embrace? We need to add the recognition that not every complaint that comes to the pastor needs to be followed; however, the call to keep it short was not an isolated complaint from an irate parishioner. It came from many arenas.

So it makes sense to consider the possibility of making the sermon more concise. Consider the possibility. Try it. Share your efforts with some trusted listeners and ask what they think about the shorter sermons. In many congregations, listeners will not be bold enough even to joke about the length of the sermon. But in congregation after congregation, listeners did report it in the interviews as a subject that matters. So we encourage preachers to attend to the length of their sermons and when in doubt, keep it short.

CHAPTER 7

Make It Plain

A story, perhaps apocryphal, tells about a well-known preacher who was asked how many points a sermon should have. "At least one," was the quick reply.

Our interviews indicate that many listeners would agree. A good sermon needs a point, a reason for being preached. Believers come to worship, hoping to hear something in the sermon, at least one thing, that will nourish their faith, challenge their behaviors, cause them to think in a new way, or stir them at a deep level. They are listening for at least one idea in the sermon to make a difference. When the experience of the sermon does not supply that for some reason, for instance because of confusing construction of the sermon, parishioners are quick to express frustration. As one listener bluntly states, "I'm here for a reason."

Although the hymns, the corporate prayers, the fellowship, and communion are spoken of highly as important parts of the service, the sermon is clearly an essential part of worship for almost all respondents. A surprising number of persons respond to the question, "What would be missing from worship if there were no sermon?" with the single, albeit grammatically incorrect, claim: "me." Without the sermon, many persons state they would simply not make the trip to church on Sunday mornings.

Since the sermon or homily is playing such a vital role in worship, it is no surprise that the listeners want to make sure they understand clearly what the preachers intend to communicate, hence the often repeated call to make the point clearly. In many African American congregations, this call is often given voice in the spontaneous congregational response as the sermon unfolds, "Make it plain, Preacher."

Respondents articulate several parts of making it plain that clarify what they hope to happen during the preaching event. By "point" they do not mean that the sermon needs to be structured with three (or so) points, but that the sermon needs to communicate a message that they can grasp and apply. This aspect extends over the time of preparation, through the delivery, and into the next week as the sermon is reflected on by the listeners. "Making it plain" is not the simple matter it may at first appear to be, so we will consider the aspects individually.

Don't Scrimp in Preparing

A surprising number of listeners report that they suspect they have heard preachers through the years who have not prepared a sermon before they step into the pulpit. Some concede the preachers may believe they are allowing the Holy Spirit more freedom if they do not bring a planned message into the sanctuary. However, most parishioners are willing to point out that the Holy Spirit can move in the pastor's study during preparation, and that preachers can allow the Spirit's assistance during delivery even if there is a full manuscript in front of them.

The minister needs to come to worship with a fully prepared sermon. Note this direct response to a request for advice for preachers: "Preparation. I think some ministers, they feel that they will be inspired by the Holy Spirit when they get there, and it will give them the message, but I would rather see them have a structure, an outline, a plan. Whatever the Holy Spirit adds to it, fine, but I don't think you ought to come up there with no preparation."

The importance of preparation is agreed on by someone from a very different congregation, who advises:

> It involves being prepared. If you're going to get up there, you have to be prepared for that hour. You have to do research and be prepared. You can't get up there and stumble through it. People are not going to accept a bumbling idiot up there. They know it's a holy time, and a lot of times it's the only hour in their life that's close to God and to get to God through those people. Being a brother of Jesus, they have to be prepared.

A third respondent, from yet another type of setting, echoes the same idea.

> Be prepared, too. The worst thing is if someone is just not prepared. When somebody just gets up there, and you never know exactly where they're trying to get. Have a purpose to your sermon. Have a point that you're trying to get to. If you can get to that where you've told somebody, "Hey. Today, this is what we'll talk about, and at the end I want you to be here," and keep that going. Have a goal and objective each sermon. Don't just get up there talking to be talking.

The issue of preparation apparently has to do with both proper study (research and prayerful thought) and composition of the sermon (having a plan, an outline, or a well-constructed manuscript to preach from).

People admit that not being adequately prepared is a significant problem, yet they sometimes are able to get past it. Note this response, in which the respect for the person of the priest was such that the poor preparation and delivery were tolerated, although it took additional effort on the part of the listener.

> I have studied communications, so an organized message is really important to me. This preacher's, they never were. And preparation. I don't think the pastor ever prepared. It just irritated the daylights out of me, but I liked the person so much. So, I worked on listening to the message.

Lest the reader think we are being unfair to preachers, we need to add that in our interviews with clergy, some admitted knowing they were not spending enough time in their sermon preparation. Although most seemed apologetic about this lack, one pastor's easy admission of cursory preparation and low regard for preaching may represent some of the problem. "But, in a way, I don't take preaching all that seriously." The same person fleshes this admission out in later comments. After describing the practice of early in the week studying the particular passage to be preached, the pastor continues: "Now most people set aside a day to write sermons, but I taught for twenty-five years. If on Saturday, I take three minutes to look at the text and have a general idea of where I want to go, and if I can have five minutes before the worship service starts on Sunday, that's all I need." The pastor goes on to explain the habit of not writing out the sermon. "What I write out is horrible. If I am in tune with myself and with the audience and just create extemporaneously, it's infinitely better." Granted this one preacher's practice is unique in our study of twenty-eight congregations (and thirty-two preachers), but we believe it represents other ministers who are serving around the country in various settings.

Much more common is the response from priests and ministers whose sermon preparation is a significant and integral part of the week's pastoral responsibilities, although quite a few admit that other demands sometimes squeeze out the sermon preparation. One rare exception is the minister whose sermon texts are planned a full year in advance and who completes drafts of sermons two weeks before preaching them. This pastor confides to the interviewer: "Preaching is my life. I live to preach."

We acknowledge that ordained ministry is a taxing vocation. The authors admit that often the many hours a person gives to a congregation seem never to be enough. However, preaching is central to what a minister does, so we pause to say as clearly as we can: In the midst of all the other demands on the priest or minister's time during the week, making adequate time for sermon preparation is an absolute necessity. Church members are aware of the importance of preparation. One listener curtly sums it up: "Know what you're talking about. Be prepared."

Some final advice to those who have not been preparing adequately comes from a layperson who has been in the church for many years. "I would say to prepare better for your next sermon. Don't bring your papers and sit down and read all through, looking for your place. Know what you're going to say." Proper preparation may begin with one's very next sermon.

It's Tough to Make It Plain

A number of listeners we interviewed tell us that preparation is connected to the preachers' ability to present the message clearly, in a way that congregants can understand easily. So both preparation and clarity of presentation are crucial. This person, for instance, notes that interrelationship: "Well, one, do their homework. Do your homework and be able to clearly articulate, 'This is what I'm trying to say to you,' and then elaborate upon it. Don't just wander." Obviously, all the preparation in the world will not matter if the message is not communicated to the gathered worshipers in a way they can comprehend. In answer to the request for final advice, a member of a small group interview was quick to say, "Be clear about what you're saying." From a very different setting comes a very similar piece of advice: "To make the word plainer. That's it. That's what I look for, how you can break God's word down and tell me what it means."

At first it may seem simple to make the message plain, yet we need to remember the diversity of persons within most congregations. In the next pages, we present some of the mixture of persons in congregations by showing the different ways people want the sermon ideas made plain. Then, in the final sections of the chapter, we report some of the suggestions from laity for communicating across the diversity in the congregation.

Ministers quickly learn that their congregations include persons who have been in the church and reading their Bibles for numerous decades, as well as those who are new to the faith and have rarely opened the Bible in their lives. Some congregants have academic degrees, while others are graduates of life's school of hard knocks. Some folks have never traveled beyond the borders of the county; some are world travelers. A sermon may seem perfectly clear to one portion of the congregation and quite murky to another. This difference is noted when several different comments about making the sermon clear are compared.

One person directs: "Put it into terms that I can understand. I'm one of those people that doesn't always get it. I've got to ask somebody sometimes to do that." Another respondent seems to agree: "Don't preach *at* me; preach *to* me. Make me take something from your sermon that I can live with and try to do. Make your point so clear that I couldn't miss if I had to trip over it." Yet, another person modifies the request somewhat, hoping for something catchy to bring the congregation on board, followed by a very defined outline that serves to make it plain.

I would say something humorous, clever, or unexpected within the first minute or two to capture my attention, and I will work to stay with the preacher for the rest of the duration. I also find it incredibly effective when I'm either told up front what to expect throughout the sermon: "I've got three points I'm going to make today. The first is What is dadadadada? My second point, dadadadada." So that I know up front where we're going, and I can sort of track the progress.

Yet another respondent is more direct about not wanting repetition. Clarity involves something other than going over and over the same point. In talking about length of sermon, this person mentions a half hour as being long enough, then moves into talking about repetition of ideas. "If you go over and over, then people are going to be tired of listening. But if you get your point across and get the sermon out in a half-hour, that's fine." A short time later, the interviewer asked for clarification about losing interest when the preacher repeats ideas. "Yes, when you keep going over it. You say it, and then I'm going to get it. Don't go back over it." Apparently, for this listener, if the preacher conveys the message clearly, once is enough. For some of the other respondents quoted above, the message needs to be communicated persistently and unambiguously, so they can be sure to "get it." Their comments translate into: Once is *not* enough.

Some listeners are able to tell exactly what the difficulty is in their understanding the sermon.

There was a sermon, and it was a very upbeat, powerful sermon— a time when you leave with an extra spring in your step—but there was no thesis statement. There was no single sentence that I could extract and say, "This is the message." I felt at times that the message was: "Gathering money, building big houses, and buying big fancy cars is okey dokey, because then people will look up to you." And I didn't feel comfortable with that at all.

When the interviewer asks what one could do in a situation like that, the same respondent continues, "I talk with others about it. I ask some folks, 'What did you hear?'…but I really felt like the omission of that one thesis statement hurt me, because I missed it." What this listener reports as "the point" heard in that sermon is almost exactly the opposite of what conversation with others reveals "the point" to have been. Because of such misunderstandings, the respondent is quite direct: "I want to hear the thesis statement early, and I want to hear it late. I want the pastor to tell me the thesis statement, and then give it to me in the sermon, and then remind me what it was so I can dial everything together and see how the parts interrelate." As a final suggestion, the same respondent adds, "I want to hear the sermon's meaning in the preacher's voice as well. I just really feel like if we don't step away hearing that point, then we're in trouble."

As if the complexity of the congregation and the different styles of listening were not enough for the preacher to have to manage, another listener lists advice for the preacher that includes a piece that seems to oppose the idea of chapter 9, "Don't Oversimplify Complex Issues." The respondent wants the preacher to "relate the sermon to anything that I can understand up front. Don't make me think too much. Don't make it complicated, I guess. So I want it said fairly simple, and yes, I do want it Bible-based, but I want it then related to what's going on now in the world." At first glance we might think such a person is eager for Christianity not to be too complicated, as if not wanting the faith to make a difference in one's life, yet this seems not to be the case at all. Rather, when the listener requests the sermon to be simple, the desire seems to be for it to be focused and unified, in order that the congregants can remember and use the message. A follow-up request is quite firm. "Give me something that I will remember later."

The desire for clarity is grounded in the belief that the sermon matters, but that it cannot matter to one's life of faith if one does not understand what the sermon intends. Several persons interviewed are aware of the need for clarity and the difficulty of making it clear to all without boring those who "get the message" easily. Some of the different suggestions people make for preachers are collected in the following sections.

Use Various Techniques

Preachers know their congregations contain a variety of listener styles and personalities. Even the most apparently homogenous group has diversity within it. The most straightforward piece of advice for preaching within such diversity is to use various techniques in preaching: varying style, for instance, from one week to the next, or making sure there are logical claims as well as images and stories to support the ideas of each sermon. However, laity are aware of the differences within their congregations. Some of the persons interviewed suggest specific ways that a preacher might engage them, so we share their reports of what helps make the message clear for them. We reproduce some of these suggestions so clergy can pay attention to them and decide to follow them as appropriate.

> I like having humor in a sermon—not lots of silly jokes, but some anecdotes are good catches to pull me into a story if there is something that can relate to actual people and real people and sort of make us laugh every now and then. Or be thoughtful. It doesn't have to be funny, I guess. Just something that you can see happening to people that you deal with on a regular basis.

The other example shows a quite different technique is needed.

> Well, as I said, I like being able to follow along. I like the nuggets. I like to be able to fill in [the outline in the bulletin] and take that

home and look at it later on and be able to discuss that with my friends that weren't able to make it that Sunday. Sometimes I feel that there is a little bit too much of "Touch three people and say, 'I am blessed.'" I think some of that is good, but too much of it kind of wears you out.

One person follows the meaning best if some humor or a thoughtful idea is used to draw the congregation in. The other person wants a fill-in-the-blanks outline in the bulletin and notes the unhelpful practice of turning to others and repeating what the preacher has said.

Laity discuss not only what helps them get the ideas in the preaching event; they also mention what helps them remember the message clearly afterwards. Again, two examples show some of the diversity of needs. "I don't think the stories are the main things that I feel are important in sermons, but they seem to be the things that help you remember the content of the sermons and the points that were made. Our priest uses childhood stories that help you link to the message of the gospel or the lessons of that day." The stories do not make the point of the sermon, but they assist in remembering the point.

Another respondent uses notes printed in the bulletin to refresh the memory of the sermon throughout the week. "They have in the program little note things. That's good. You can read it before you start your day or whatever. Just so the preacher can make it really clear. Like I said, use examples for today so you can remember it." These various listeners are actually revealing what they need to receive the message clearly and to remember it throughout the upcoming week. Preachers could benefit from listening to them.

Laity are often able to offer direct insight and advice for ministers facing this inevitable situation of a congregation of diverse listeners who are all eager for the preacher to make the point clearly. Consider this assessment from an interview with a teenager. "Some people can't learn by somebody just standing up there talking. Some people learn by watching. Some people learn by movement. Some people learn by little flashcards. Reverend could have a note in the bulletin, could have a little acting at the part before the sermon. Things like that, because everybody learns differently and understands differently." What the teen is advising is for the preacher to use a variety of techniques to make the point clear and to assist the congregation in remembering the message.

Stick to a Single Point

An important point to note in the requests to use various techniques is the assumption that the preacher will nonetheless keep the sermon focused. Those we interviewed do not encourage the preacher to make a variety of points or to try to say a number of things to please all the different types of listeners. They suggest using various techniques to help people comprehend the main ideas or point or message of the sermon. Many of the interview respondents express a deeply held opinion that the preacher needs to have a specific focus clearly in mind. Here is a sampling: "For heaven's sake, do not have too many points. I just get so irritated when there's too many points and not enough thought. That's a chief frustration as far as content is concerned."

From a different denomination in a very different setting, another respondent offers: "Stay on one topic or area. You can always talk about something else the next week. We'll still be there."

Another respondent agrees, advising: "One thing would be to stick to the topic. Develop the sermon. Don't just ramble. Stick to whatever the point is at that particular time. To make it and then sit down." And another person echoes the idea: "A simple message. Stick to the text. Have a central message, just one. Preachers put two or three or four or five or six different ideas in one sermon. They've actually got five sermons. Then it loses the acuteness of the message. If you can contain yourself, you'll do better."

A final comment comes from a small group interview: "I have heard sermons from preachers that I did not understand. The ones I didn't understand seemed like they were bouncing around a whole lot. Our pastor, it seems like our pastor is on line. The sermon stays with the same subject even as it brings in another story to try to get the same point across. You still understand what our minister is trying to say." These quite similar pieces of advice in this section come from five different congregations, four different denominations, both African American and Anglo congregations; although all women, they come from city and small town settings. Focus seems a crucial ingredient for listeners no matter what the setting.

We provide two additional comments from interviewees who confirm appreciation for sermons that keep their focus. "I appreciate ministers who have organized minds that then correlate their sermons. They're easy to follow. They don't get off on tangents and talk about things that don't have anything to do with what they are talking about." The other also expresses gratitude for sermons that stick to a single topic. "I like sermons that come to the pulpit, and there's a focus there, and there's an idea, and it's developed. That's what I like. A sermon that causes you to think differently. Gives you something to think about that you just had not, I never thought of it that way."

Something for the Week

Although several of the quotations cited above already reveal a significant desire for the sermon to leave the congregation with something to nourish them through the week, we underline the importance of this need. The call for a clear focus does not in any way indicate the congregation's desire for a message that is thin or overly simplistic. We recall no one interviewed who treated the sermon as a piece unimportant to their faith; quite the contrary. Persons were eager for the sermon to be focused enough to be meaningful, as if understanding the need for what we might call "bite-sized" pieces of the faith.

Carrying this analogy further, quite a few persons called for the sermon to give them something to "chew on" for the week ahead. So we might say people wanted to have spiritual nourishment from the sermon that was small enough to ingest, yet significant enough to feed them during the week ahead. So we share here a few comments about sermons as "food for later thought" from respondents in various congregational settings. "The sermon gives us a basis for discussion at home around spiritual issues in a different way." A listener in a congregation that uses an outline in the bulletin notes a similar appreciation for considering sermon ideas later:

> You take that home, because my family has been writing the same thing down. Then, in the car, we can pull it out, and we have something we can go back to. "Remember when the priest said this?" "What did you think about that?" The teaching time can continue. What I like about it is, our thoughts are going to be organized the same way to talk about it later. That's very helpful.

One final comment from a person who is interested in the sermon not merely being something to think about for the next week, but something functional, practical to the faith: "I like for it to be something that can be applied to one's daily life, and as you leave you feel like it's something that you can truly use."

Without doubt those who gather into pews Sunday after Sunday are waiting for their preachers to share a word about the faith that they can hear and understand clearly. Although many are gracious about sermons that are less than plain, and many recognize the multiple challenges of communicating a message clearly, they remain hopeful that preachers will continue to work on making their sermonic points clearly.

CHAPTER 8
_____

Talk about Everything

In gatherings of clergy, we sometimes hear preachers say they are reluctant to talk about certain things from the pulpit because they fear that the congregation will respond negatively. Subjects they are hesitant to address often concern politics, sexuality, and matters of social justice. Occasionally, ministers fear not only that the congregation will be aggravated (and perhaps stop attending church), but that the congregation will fire them. While the individuals and groups interviewed for this study do not speak with one voice on this matter, most of the laity who speak about it agree. Not only *can* preachers "talk about everything," but they also *should* do so. Of course, some people think that some issues should be off-limits to preaching, and even some of those who say that sermons could be "about everything" qualify their remarks.

In this chapter we first listen to some respondents affirm that the preacher can and even should bring a wide range of issues into the pulpit. We trace the rationales that such listeners offer for this wide-ranging focus and ponder the fact that many people say they *want* guidance from the pulpit in making sense of life, including on topics that are sensitive and difficult. We note that many folk see positive values in the preacher speaking about things that may make the congregation uncomfortable. A significant number of interviewees call for preachers to be honest about what they really think—even about controversial issues. They suggest some things that preachers can do when preaching on such subjects. A preacher, of course, needs to be ready for diverse reactions to sermons on a wide variety of issues.

Preach the Range of Life Issues

The interviewers asked, "Do you think there are some issues that are too explosive to talk about from the pulpit?" The vast majority of people answered, "No." Many preachers, including the members of the project team, were surprised by the fact that so many people gave this response and with such great conviction. The following responses are representative.

One person says, simply, "If you can't bring issues up, then the church is not doing what it is supposed to do." In this vein, another person laments that the legal world named child molestation as an important issue and took steps to protect children before the church did. "It was like sometimes, we just shut the doors, and we don't want to talk about certain issues."

When asked if any topics are too controversial for a sermon, a small group interview from a representative church says:

INTERVIEWEE 1: Everything is fair game.
INTERVIEWEE 2: I think so, too.
INTERVIEWEE 3: This is life.
INTERVIEWEE 4: Same as life and should be preached from the pulpit.

A similar dialogue in a small group in another congregation makes the explicit qualification that ministers can preach about anything "as long as they are preaching the Word."

Referring to the specific issue of homosexuality, a small group in another community comes to a similar conclusion.

INTERVIEWEE 1: Are there any large issues that should not be addressed? I don't think so. Again I come to this, but the issue of homosexuality in the church. I find it problematic that our denomination is still wrestling with this when a number of other denominations have been able to put this to bed. What we've been trying to do is straddle the fence here, and I'm pretty sure I know where our pastors would come down on this issue. I'm not one hundred per cent sure; but, nevertheless, things like that are often avoided. It's not the only thing that's avoided, and I don't think we're well served by doing that. There may be times—and I think we're not as sensitive to this as we could be—where we might want to have adult sermons.
INTERVIEWEE 2: The ministers try to make everything pretty G-rated.
INTERVIEWEE 3: But life isn't like that.

Below, we note that some congregations have "adult sermons," that is, sermons in which children and young people exit the sanctuary, leaving the adults to talk about sensitive matters.

The people who offer a rationale for preaching on the wide range of life's issues do so with basic and direct reasons. The most commonly articulated reason is that the Bible deals with the wide spectrum of issues. "Because every situation happens in the Bible, then it should be discussed in the pulpit. There's nothing that's going to happen that hasn't happened. So, to me, I think everything should be preached or touched upon because at some point it's going to hit somebody."

Other people offer a similar rationale with respect to the approach that Jesus took to issues that need to be addressed. "Things got to that point where people didn't talk about things, where it was, 'That's not polite or appropriate.' Christ wasn't always polite or appropriate." Another person speaks similarly, "I think being able to preach on dangerous topics goes back to the Bible as your core belief, that Jesus tackled these tough issues, and so, therefore, we should."

Other congregants are conscious of needing assistance in thinking theologically about important matters. Of homosexuality and divorce, "and issues that have been around for hundreds of years, we need to hear about them and not skirt around them. In my opinion we don't hear about them. What am I looking for? Help."

For others, public discussion is a way to deal with difficulties in community. Of homosexuality and racial ethnic segregation, one hearer says, "We're not going to solve the problem if you don't talk about it. If you don't bring things out in the open and discuss them, you're never going to be able to solve any problem if you just ignore it." A different voice adds, "If you're going to live your religion, then you're going to have to incorporate it into your life. I don't see any reason why you shouldn't talk about these things."

In a small group experience, the people agreed that one reason for their congregation's growth is the fact that "there are no taboo subjects here. The pastor will go through the whole gamut. This pastor will go through the whole Bible."

Seeking Theological Guidance

Many of the people interviewed for this project explicitly say they seek theological guidance from the preacher on the wide range of life's issues. Though some do not use the term "theology," they desire to understand life theologically, that is, from the perspective of their deepest convictions about God. This desire comes through the following quote.

I really think everything should be talked about from the pulpit, but I think it should be talked about in the context of what God says, not what we want, not what we say. It's really what God says that's important. What I think about it, if it doesn't line up with what God says about it, then I better start changing the way I think about it. [Certain well known preachers] have been very direct, including everything from racism to sex to everything, very direct and very scriptural, which I think is wonderful. So I don't shy away from any of it, but I want it to be in relation, in context with what God says, not what human beings say, not what somebody's idea should be politically correct.

This listener seems to assume that one can know "what God says" by simply turning to the Bible. Others who do not agree with that position on the

Bible would still join this person in wanting the sermon to help them understand life from a transcendent perspective.

The interviews are rife with similar statements of desire on the part of parishioners for the sermon to help them make theological sense of life. We hear this theme in the following quotes that come from a variety of listeners. One says,

> I think the sermon challenges. It stimulates people to examine themselves spiritually and emotionally. I think that's usually been our preacher's goal—to challenge people to reevaluate their lives and look at all the barriers that maybe get in the way of living the kind of life, the godly life, they would like to live. Have a greater conscious contact with God and what gets in the way of that. So, looking at those issues—I think we're challenged with that here. I think our minister does a nice job in challenging people.

Similar themes come out in the following quote from a different congregation.

> I'm hoping there will be a message brought to share God's love, to reinforce that in your life and to go out and live it in your daily living. To help you know that you're not alone whatever you face on Monday morning. Yet, at the same time remind you that you have a responsibility, that God has expectations of us. Out of all these expectations, God still loves us in spite of ourselves.

Someone from another church puts this concern concisely in response to the question, "Do you think there are some issues that are just too explosive or too dangerous to be discussed by a preacher from the pulpit?" The interviewee replies, "No. I tend to think those are probably more enlightening. Sometimes you really need to hear that controversial thing to come to grips with it and deal with it." Another person reinforces:

> This is the real world we live in, and all those horrible, terrible things that are out there is the world that we're living in. You can't sweep that under the rug. You've got to bring it out in the open and talk about it. I think sometimes there's no better forum than the church to start talking about those probing issues and those hard topics that are difficult to discuss.

Thinking about Things the Congregation Does Not Want to Think about

Several parishioners report of their preachers, "They make us think about things we may not want to think about." These listeners contend that the preachers sometimes need to press the congregation to think about such matters when doing so helps the congregation consider matters they might prefer to avoid. "They make you think. They have connectivity to current events. They may make you think about things that you may or may not want to think about. Then they connect it to the Word of God."

A question was put to one listener, "What do you think that preaching does in this congregation that other things do not do?"

> It gets many of the people in the same room thinking about the same topic—the ones who aren't whacking the kids on top of the head during the sermon. But you do get a commonality of purpose for a short time, and that's very good. The other thing is that sometimes—and this does not happen every time—sometimes you get those people thinking about something they don't really want to think about, and I think that is, in its own way, just as valid.

In a similar mood someone else avers, "If you don't step on a few toes and make people uncomfortable, then I feel a preacher is not doing the job. If they don't give somebody something to stir their soul, they haven't done enough."

A couple of listeners notice that their pastors do not always preach "feel good" sermons. They like the fact that these messages are "sermons in which you have to think about it."

INTERVIEWEE 1: The TV preachers and the doomsday discussions and the discussions that if you just follow Christ, your life will be wonderful. There won't be any problems. You will have diamond rings.
INTERVIEWEE 2: Your husband will love you.
INTERVIEWEE 3: That's right. If you just follow Christ, everything will be good. I have trouble, I guess, with such feel good sermons.

Another listener concludes this phase of the discussion by saying, "You know you can't feel good all the time. You know that's not life and that's not real." These listeners want the preacher to help them discern God's presence in helping them make their way through the ambiguities of life.

Be Honest about What You Really Think

The parishioners in the research congregations put out a persistent call for preachers to state what they really think about the central concerns of the sermon.

INTERVIEWEE 1: I can think of something that de-energizes me. So that is what not to do. It's this filtering we talked about earlier [i.e., the preacher filtering out sensitive topics]. Tell us what you think. Don't hold back.
INTERVIEWEE 2: Lay it all out.
INTERVIEWEE 3: Lay it all out. Don't feel like you've got to hold back. If you're inhibited, trust me; all the eyes in the congregation can see that you're holding back.

Echoing other themes in this chapter, one crisp thinker in the interview population says:

> Approach life from an honest standpoint. Don't pull punches. Talk about the difficult things. Bring them up. Try to relate them to what God's will would be as far as these difficult topics that we have to face. Be brave. Don't back off from things. Be truthful. Don't just say what you think the congregation would want you to say. It may not be practical, but that's what I would prefer that they be.

This hearer concludes, "Talk about the tough things in life. Bring them up."

For at least one listener, the desire for honesty extends as far as the minister not preaching when the sermonic well has been dry.

> I like the fact that the minister is honest. This is one of the things that comes up when you talk about sermons. There've been occasions when the minister's got in the pulpit and said, "Absolutely nothing pulled my chain this week," and there's no sermon. I'll ask the reason. "What happened?" The minister will say, "I just couldn't get fired up." As a teacher, I can appreciate that because there are times when I go in for a lecture and just nothing is falling into place. When I get about twenty minutes into that kind of class, I just say, "Go away. You're wasting your time sitting here because I don't have any idea what I'm doing today." That kind of honesty is really appreciated.

Reservations about Bringing "Everything" into the Pulpit

Although many listeners initially say they think that the preacher should be able to talk about anything in the pulpit, some of these same folk have second thoughts and admit that they think a preacher might not want to bring some things into the pulpit. Some ideas or situations seem inappropriate or distracting.

Several listeners indicate that they are distracted when preachers bring their own experience directly into the pulpit every Sunday. One interviewee does not go to worship "every Sunday to hear what the minister has to say about his or her own personal life, but to relate it to the congregation. A preacher can do that in a lot of ways." Another congregant makes a similar point with respect to preachers who return again and again to the same themes in sermons. "If there is an issue that really sits with the preacher, I don't think it should be harped on every Sunday, like a personal issue. I think that should all be gone. The sermon ought to come from the Word of God." These congregants do want to hear about the preacher's experience, but not every week, and in a context in which ministers use their experience as a lens to help the congregation move toward a theological interpretation of life.

Another common reservation, which we discuss in more detail toward the end of chapter 3, concerns the sermon involving intimate details from the preacher's own life or similar details from the lives of others. "There are personal things, and they need to stay personal."

Some interviewees discourage preachers from endorsing particular political parties or candidates. One person says, "If they try to say, 'If you don't vote this way, you're not a Christian,' I have a problem whenever I hear that. I cringe when they get up in the pulpit and do that." This reservation needs some qualification, however, as some listeners seek general guidance in how to think theologically about the world of politics even when they do not want the preacher to make partisan recommendations concerning candidates for whom to vote. "I don't want them to be up there and be politicians, but I want to learn about what is right and wrong." Another hearer says, "Current issues would be tough to touch, but they need to be touched upon. Here it would be touched upon for you to make your own decision. 'Here is the issue, and here is how it related to scripture.' Then it's up to you."

Some Suggestions for Preaching on Controversial Subjects

In the midst of commenting on other things, several listeners volunteer qualities preachers can bring into sermons to help congregations engage sensitive subjects. These ideas do not constitute a complete approach to preaching on challenging issues, but they are suggestive.[1]

The preacher's attitude is a key for several people. One person reports: "Our pastor knows this congregation pretty well. If the pastor is going to bring up something that could be explosive, the pastor will put it in such a way that is not so explosive. The way the pastor approaches it is nonthreatening to either side but puts it on the table in such a way that we can discuss it."

A member of another church gives an example of how the preacher got into a sermon on an aspect of sexuality. This pastor preached

> ...in love, not in a judgmental way. The fact that the minister tries is part of that, too, so it doesn't seem so judgmental. Preaching about homosexuality, the minister says, "I'm going to tell you what the Bible says. You may not like what the Bible says, but here's what it says. I'm not being any more judgmental about this than I am about all the other sins that are in the Bible. I'm going to preach it in love."

Readers who have a different theological interpretation of homosexuality from the one assumed by this preacher and interviewee can still note the preacher's attitude: the preacher does not begin with a judgmental claim but with an invitation to a thoughtful conversation.

Other listeners point out that such a sermon "has got to be done by somebody who knows what they're doing and is very well prepared. This is not for the faint of heart." Other listeners recommend giving "both sides of the topic." For example, one interviewee says, "What the preacher should do is try to bring a better understanding of the two polarized opinions so that you can appreciate the other person's opinion."

Another congregant, who leads a Bible study group in a congregation, approvingly compares the instructional style used in the study group with the preacher's approach to challenging issues. "I guess from my teaching background, I try to take points like that, and I try to gather information from both sides, rather than just getting the people over on my side to agree about that and not looking at the other side. I appreciate the preacher's viewpoint even though that might not be the same as mine." Out of such differences, another hearer expects "that I will learn something, that I will grow. It will be a means to grow. That I will experience God. I don't expect to always agree. Out of that difference, it may present opportunities to talk about that." When a message articulates the multiple sides of an issue, listeners understand each point of view and the reasoning behind it. Such data is necessary for responsible critical thinking, as many listeners indicate.

Occasionally, respondents recommend giving parents the opportunity to take children out of the worship space when the subject matter of the sermon may not be appropriate for certain ages. For example, "'Today,' the preacher said, 'In this particular part of my marriage series, I'm going to talk about intimacy. I think it would be appropriate to take your children to the children's program. I'm not sure you're going to feel comfortable with them hearing some of the things I have to say.'" A listener from another church speaks of this practice as "an adult sermon" where we "would set up a separate children's session and we [in the worship space] would talk about something that was really for eighteen and older."

Be Ready for Diverse Reactions

Several congregants caution the preacher to recognize that sermons will not always create unanimity of viewpoint in the community. Indeed, in this matter, as in so many others in this exploration, diversity is a watchword. "I don't know that you'll ever get an acceptance of a hundred percent, but I guess that's why we have so many denominations. People don't agree." Another response is similar but fuller.

I'd say, "Don't be afraid to say something that might give you negative feedback just because some people might think otherwise." Everybody thinks differently…Everybody thinks differently. I don't know if it's ever the case that everybody agrees. I imagine some people are afraid when people come up and maybe say they didn't like the sermon, or it was in bad taste or something, but I think it gets people to thinking. Just because one person is upset doesn't mean everybody is.

Even when this interviewee does disagree with the preacher's point, "I just try to understand what they're trying to say. Everybody is different."

Most of the people who reflected on how their congregations respond to sermons on challenging subjects said something like the following. "The congregation has enough open-minded people that these issues would be something that everybody could talk about. They may not all agree on how to approach it or how to deal with it, but I think we could all sit around this table and say, 'Okay, I see your point, but I do not agree with it.'" This attitude is at least partly the result of ministerial leadership. "Our pastor just kind of has that influence over the congregation." That is, the pastor influences the congregation to listen to others and to appreciate their diversity.

In an interview that took place a couple of months after the destruction of the World Trade Towers on September 11, 2001, an interviewee gives an account of a sermon that ties together much of this chapter.

> About three or four weeks ago, our pastor did a sermon focused on how we react to that event. I thought it was a little early to put that idea on the table, but this is our pastor. Our needs are to be more forgiving. It's a time when we haven't bombed anybody yet or done anything. As Christians we really need to think about this: at some point in time, we're going to have to forgive—in spite of 5,000 people being dead in New York and changing all our lives. I thought that sermon took a lot of guts. It's one of the sermons that really stuck with me.

For this listener, as for several others in the sample group, sermons on difficult issues are some of the most engaging, memorable, and helpful. We hope that such testimony will empower preachers to bring the full range of life issues into the pulpit for theological consideration.

CHAPTER 9
_____

Don't Oversimplify
Complex Issues

Here is a true story. Five ministers sat at their weekly lectionary study group discussing what they were going to preach the next Sunday. They represented five congregations of three different denominations. The person presenting the material about the passage from the book of Exodus excitedly began to talk about a possible sermon on the text. The other four faces at the table showed surprise. Finally, one said something like this: "I never preach on the Old Testament. It would take me twenty minutes to explain the context of the book and another twenty minutes to explain the specific setting of this passage. They'd still never get it, and I'd never get to the sermon." Clearly this pastor believed the congregation was not familiar enough with the Bible to understand the parts written before the birth of Jesus, and also that people listening to a sermon on those passages could not be taught how they were important. Laity from various settings disagree with this preacher's assessment.

Those who frequently listen to sermons seem quite eager to learn as much as they can about the faith, not only the history of the ancestors (all of them), but also how we are to comprehend biblical literature for spiritual and ethical assistance for the life of faith today. People understand that the modern world is a complicated place. One's religion necessarily needs to be complex to address it. Laity are often quite willing to have clergy work with them, even lead them, as they consider the complexities of the faith. What they do not want is a simplistic presentation of the faith. This chapter looks at the listeners' request to preachers: Don't oversimplify complex issues.

We Aren't Dummies

Representatives from various congregations are quick to raise a complaint when preachers act as if they have to "dumb down" the faith to make it comprehensible to the average person sitting in the pew. Members talking with our interviewers discuss reactions to radio and television preachers, reading books about the faith, and, most importantly, thinking about how their Christianity should and does influence their lives. Preachers need to realize that people who come to worship want to hear something fresh about the faith, and their listeners are bright enough to comprehend ideas presented well from the pulpit. Many members of the laity want to be invited to a new depth of living out what they believe.

Consider the listener from an urban, liturgical congregation, who urges the preacher not to treat the congregation as if they do not know what is going on. The appeal is to teach the congregation something new: "I think, again, just don't sell the congregation short. If you had a bad week and you just didn't have a chance to prepare, that's fine, but don't think people don't realize it. If you invest yourself in preparation and invest yourself in trying to take the group to a new place, that will also be appreciated, even if people disagree." People can disagree with the preacher and the roof does not fall in, and they do not ride the preacher out of town on a rail. Instead, they appreciate not being treated as if they are ignorant.

Another listener, from a nonliturgical congregation in a more rural setting, shares many of the same thoughts: "So I need the preacher to maybe hit a few main points, because as a listener, that's what I can hold onto. If you have a thin sermon topic, I'm not going to be able to hold on, and frankly, I'm going to become discouraged trying to keep that all together. If you have two to four points, I can follow those points, and I can stay with you."

Congregants perceive preachers who oversimplify the faith as treating them as if they are not bright enough to consider more complex ideas. Coming under particularly stiff criticism are preachers who act as if just getting people in the door is enough, so it does not matter how watered down the sermon ideas are presented. Such preaching copies the "numbers game" of society at large and is considered empty by some listeners, because it allows people to consider themselves believers without requiring any change.

> Today you've got all sorts of competition. It's tough. That's why these churches focusing on huge numbers and a specific organization model and so forth, they've copied all this cheap stuff from modern culture and tried to beat people at their own game. I wouldn't want it. If it's successful, what's it successful at doing? Just getting them in? Yes, you can grab people where they are, but you don't want to be where they are. You want them to be someplace else.

In explaining that they are not dummies, congregants point out various ways they have acquired sophisticated ideas. Several examples are given in the next section.

Our Faith Can Be Sophisticated without Being Obscure

When students walk into second year Spanish class, the teacher expects they have had first year. Students would be insulted if the teacher began as if they knew nothing. On the other hand, the first year class would be confounded if the teacher began with second year lessons. We humans are able to progress through complicated ideas and information when we are brought along step by step. Christian faith is not as simple as learning to translate one language into another (as difficult as that is for some of us), but the analogy is apt. We learn the faith when ideas build on one another. Weekly sermons can be a significant part of the understanding and development of the life of faith.

Listeners praise some preachers for helping bring them along in their comprehension of the Christian faith life and mention other ways they have grown in the faith irrespective of their preachers' sermons.

> Good preachers need to study and take the membership to a deeper depth. This is just my own personal belief. I often think that some ministers don't believe that there are laypersons who actually study. I don't want to hear shallow preaching. I want to hear in-depth preaching, because I do study. I can differentiate if someone says something that's not true. I know that right away what they said is not true. If I'm questioning, I'm going to go home and I'm going to look it up for myself just to know.

Many lay people study on their own, evaluate claims the minister may make, and work to utilize new ideas. They appreciate when the preacher assists in the process. One person puts it quite plainly. "A sermon gives me sometimes the framework or the words to be able to play with new knowledge, so that I can take ownership of that knowledge." Note how the listener is not just interested in playing with new knowledge, but in spending time making those new ideas part of her or his own faith.

Sermon information is appreciated when it helps people grow in their spirituality. And it is not appreciated when the sermon oversimplifies the faith life, as shown in the response by this person: "Second of all, give me credit for being able to handle abstract, sophisticated thought. A lot of messages really are simple. God is love. Where do you go from there? Let's shake hands and go home? We've just covered the topic? But I think that sells your congregation short." The answer goes on to advise preachers to present more sophisticated ideas in their sermons:

> Be willing to step up and say, "Hey, let's talk about church leaders who favor full inclusion of gay men and lesbians." Be willing to

admit, "I'm not really sure what I think of their ideas." Okay? I can listen to both sides of that. And let's talk about Process Theology. Let's talk about the Historical Jesus Movement, abortion, homosexuality, or whatever; something that's potentially disturbing to folks. Let's go back to an example of a potentially explosive topic that was handled very, very well in our pulpit. The preacher said, "Here is a set of views. Here is stuff I want you to think about. My fundamental message is this." It was handled nicely. I walked away having learned new things in a challenging way, and it didn't do me a whole heck of a lot of harm.

In further explanation of ways the preacher assists teaching and challenging the congregation in various arenas of the faith, this same respondent speaks of the priest's ability to acknowledge the intelligence of the congregation. "I think something that was potentially emotional was approached in a very professorial way, in a very academic way, respecting that there was an emotional aspect to it. Again, that goes back to treating your congregation as adults and recognizing the intellect of the congregation." The importance of honoring the intellect of the congregation is echoed in another response. "For me, the best would be to be thought-provoking, yet nonprescriptive, and to not separate the spiritual from the intellectual."

Some listeners give specific topics or ideas the preacher could address in more sophisticated ways. One of the youngest of our respondents speaks of the confusion that results from trying to make sense of what the school system teaches and what one hears from the pulpit. Science class, in the respondent's academically advanced high school, gives detailed information about the make-up of the universe. In worship, sermons do not address these issues with enough complexity or detail to satisfy the faith questions. The young person continues: "I get confused sometimes. I don't want to tell people this, because then they start bringing up some other stuff that's not answering my question. That's what I really wanted to know, how everything started."

Sermons that merely claim that God created the universe are not enough for this young mind. We hear in this young Christian's question one of the most ancient queries of philosophical minds: Why is there *something* rather than *nothing*? This young worshiper, like others of various ages in congregations around the country, is able to handle more about the faith than is being offered from the pulpit.

One response may reveal a concern that makes the appeal for more depth to preaching more urgent. "The time for playing and trying to please people with their sermons and all that is over. We need to hear what God wants us to hear." The person seems to be saying, if preachers are not sharing the faith fully with their congregations, people are not being told what it is God wants them to know. If we think about it, this is a very serious situation. Because they are not sure the congregations can handle the faith fully, clergy are watering down or withholding certain parts of God's message.

We want to be quick to point out that some congregants praise their ministers for doing exactly what others neglect, namely preaching with a depth that honors both the intelligence of the congregation and the importance of the faith for life today. In answering the question about what makes for an engaging sermon, one small group discusses appreciation for their preacher's ability to share new insights about sensitive subjects or unfamiliar scripture passages. "To me, any sermon is engaging that would have controversy or a passage that nobody else would have picked. 'Why would this be so?' I cannot think of a reason, but our preacher brings about a reason. The sermons here do it quite often actually. Our preacher does not usually have the 'feel-good sermon.'"

Although some individuals and small groups easily discuss how their priests and ministers preach in ways that assist growing in the faith, others quite pointedly claim preachers underestimate their ability to comprehend more complex faith ideas.

Preachers Underestimate Us

Perhaps because many clergy persons have attended seminary, they take care that their sermons are not too complicated for the average church member to understand. Better to err on the side of simplicity than to speak in language too esoteric for normal comprehension. However, this tendency toward simplicity and clarity sometimes translates into sermons pitched simplistically, denying the typical congregation's ability to grow and build on ideas from week to week and even year to year.

Many congregants are aware that they could be learning more. One person interviewed is ready to pass on some thoughts to preachers. "Sometimes a preacher will preach or sing or whoop or whatever to get people all worked up. After that's over with and done, they leave and there's nothing there. But when you've actually heard the word from the Lord, that's when you go home and your lives are changed. That's what makes a difference. I would tell them all those things." Apparently having something left after the sermon, especially something that changes one's life, is a clue that a sermon has contained a word from God.

When preachers do not use the sermon to communicate the deeper concepts of the faith, listeners are aware they are not getting fully what they need. Hear this person's belief that congregants are inarticulate because preachers tell stories but do not teach the faith fully.

> I think it's real important to have the congregation grounded in the scripture. I think a lot of pastors don't do that. They give a lot of feel good stories, but they're not grounded. I don't think that's

the primary purpose of preaching, but I think that's one of the purposes of preaching—that they're grounded, to know why you believe what you believe. Somebody comes along telling you, you don't have to believe in the resurrection. Then the congregation needs to know why we believe in the resurrection. Every now and then the preacher needs to preach on that and some of the core issues.

This idea is echoed in other responses from various settings. People want to be able to know what the core Christian beliefs are and how to defend them when questioned.

Many persons express the desire for preachers to help them become more mature in the faith and more knowledgeable about scripture, history, and the contemporary significance of Christianity. For instance, here is a person of a different gender, denomination, congregation size, and setting: "Have a good base for what you're talking about. Well, I don't want to say 'don't assume we know everything,' but I want to say 'take people to a little bit higher level than you think they could go.'"

Some respondents give specific examples of sermons that left them feeling like the preacher had not given them all that they needed. In a small group, one person reports on a sermon that attempted to frighten people into heaven by showing them the terrors of hell:

I'll tell you what it did. It took me so far to hell I couldn't get hell out of my mind and see the salvation, which was what the preacher was trying to say. But the salvation was not there. If I had not known God, the love of Jesus, I would have been like this: "Where's the hope?" I could have left as a sinner and not given my life to Christ. I could have left in fear, because what was being said overpowered the love of Christ.

Another person in the group agrees: "The only thing you could think of was fear."

Similarly, a teenage listener reports a specific sermon that was troubling: "Sex. Reverend talks about sex and when you should do it. You can't tell when a person is ready. Our minister pressed waiting on a lot of females. That's one thing I think the Reverend shouldn't talk about as much, because he's male. He doesn't understand what goes on with teens nowadays about that stuff." The respondent senses something is wrong with such directives in sermons, yet is not fully able to articulate what it is, other than when male preachers direct young women (and apparently only the women) to wait for sex, it feels inappropriate since the ministers are male and older. Apparently, sermons that merely pronounce a judgment are not going to be as well received.

A final example of preachers' underestimating the congregations' ability to comprehend more complex subjects and ideas comes from a person who wishes the minister would tackle some political issues:

> I have always wondered why Pastor doesn't approach politics somewhat. Now we are all involved in politics. We're all voters. We're concerned about the direction of the country. That seems to be one hot button that our preacher will not touch. It's always bothered me a little bit that ours wouldn't, because I think that's exactly what a pastor should be doing."

Sometimes preachers demonstrate they are underestimating a congregation's ability by neglecting to be careful about consistency of thought from week to week. It appears such erratic and therefore unreliable content is heard to show a lack of concern by the preacher. "Stand your ground. You will lose people's respect in a sermon by preaching something this way and then next week flipping it this way, because it pacifies a certain...Be sure of what you say, and don't contradict yourself."

Respondents are able to see that more complicated sermons that show the depth of ideas will sometimes be difficult, even trying, within the congregation. Yet, many seem to prefer this to simpler sermons that truncate the faith. In a small group interview, appreciation is expressed for the preacher's willingness to allow for depth and disagreement that is not tidy, but does result in people's maturation as individuals and as a community in the faith. "In some cases, preaching on explosive issues can bring us a little bit closer together as a congregation. I think that's necessary. It may not always be pretty, and people are going to cry. I'm sure I've been one of those people a couple times. I think our pastor needs to challenge people. I think they need to be challenging sermons." Another person adds a comment about those sermons on hot topics: "I think our minister has hit them all." When preachers are willing to take the congregation onto new ground, many persons appreciate it.

Some of Us Want It Simple

Our interviewees do not speak with a singular voice about wanting more sophisticated sermons. A few seem to say almost the opposite.For instance, recollect the interviewee who, on page 68, is quoted as saying, "Don't make me think too much. Don't make it complicated, I guess. So I want it said fairly simple." We cannot tell if this final piece of advice actually means the speaker wants to hear the same level of message year after year or that the speaker wants any new information or ideas in the sermon to build slowly from their current firm foundation.

Another comment sounds a similar note and reminds us of the entire chapter on making the point clearly. "Try not to get real deep, to extrapolate too far. Make some examples, but keep it simple." As we learn in chapter 7, often people want sermons to be focused and explained plainly. This does not necessarily preclude a gradual movement into deeper waters. Simple ideas, slowly building on other simple ideas, can move the congregation to new places in the faith. However, it is difficult to know whether these few respondents who call for keeping the sermons "simple" or "uncomplicated" actually mean they want the sermon to reinforce ideas they already know and do not want to move to more sophisticated or deeper understandings. Perhaps they really do want sermons that enable them to stay right where they are.

Open Up Subjects

Although not universal, many of the persons we interviewed express appreciation for sermons that show new ways to think about the faith and present new ideas about living the Christian life. One of the most concise answers says it well: "Leave room for thinking. Don't close the subject; open it up." The sense of wanting various areas of the faith "opened up" is raised again and again. Many people want the preacher to share information to help them reach their own conclusions rather than having the preacher tell them what to think.

A small group discussion confirms this idea. One person notes: "Our pastors have been careful to provide both sides and provide a language, a context in which we can discuss these things." Another person in the group gives an additional ingredient. "Reverend almost always starts the sermon with questions that the sermon is intended to address—not answer, but address."

The group also expresses appreciation for the minister's ability to discuss topics without having to have the final word. Priests and ministers might take a word of comfort and advice from the members of this small group conversation, for they express appreciation for their preacher's willingness to assist their consideration of many topics without needing to provide definitive answers. Group members mention examples of sermons that specifically brought up sexuality, singleness, homosexuality, the "fatherhood of God," gossip, kids in worship, and adultery. Such sermons give congregants the opportunity to think through these issues in the proper setting.

Appreciation for not having to have the last word does not necessarily imply congregants do not want the preacher to have an opinion. On the contrary, respondents often express a desire to know what the preacher believes is correct. Consider this response:

> Stand for something. Don't be wishy-washy. Don't beat around the bush. Stand for something. Some things in life are good. Some things in life are bad. Some things in life are neither. They simply are. But don't be afraid to say, "This is how it is. God wants us to

feed people. God wants us to clothe people. God wants us to love one another and to help one another." I think too many times we're afraid of stepping on toes. If I were going to tell them anything to energize me, it's, "Don't be afraid to take a stand."

Apparently many listeners *do* want their preachers to teach the faith and express their opinions. For example, the interviewee cited on page 78 made this very point. "Talk about the tough things in life. Bring them up."

These ideas are key. People are game to hear these topics discussed, to have the language provided for thinking them through, but they also appreciate the clergy's ability to treat the congregations as being intelligent enough to make decisions for themselves.

Several preachers were commended for the way they opened up thinking after the events of September 11, 2001. Most often the preachers' ability to acknowledge that these events could not be addressed with easy "stock answers" was held as particularly praiseworthy. Several respondents indicated that the preachers' comments developed over several weeks, indicating continued thinking and maturation of thought about complex issues. In a small group, one person speaks in detail about the sermon the Sunday following September 11, 2001. After reciting the title, the respondent continues:

> Our preacher was just talking about how it was okay to be an American, and then also it was okay to be a Christian and a member of a historic peace church. Someone handed our pastor a pin to put on that's red, white, and blue, but then somebody else gave a pin of the world and a peace sign or something like that. The sermon was talking about how those two can coexist. That was really helpful for me. I think a lot of people need that.

In another congregation, the preacher devoted several weeks to considering the events. One member recited part of the sermon of the first week, then talked of how the minister's ideas evolved in the following weeks, and how the pulpit was made available to a member of the congregation with another position. The respondent notes: "I think that's a sign of a very healthy church actually. The preacher is big enough to do that." Several comments later, the respondent concludes: "I felt our preacher was fulfilling a valuable function. It was a means of working through this."

Implied in the comments about the preachers' ability to express strong opinions, give information, and allow the congregation to think through issues on its own is appreciation for the preachers' treating their congregations as made up of intelligent adults, able to learn and grow in the faith. These are priests and ministers who are not oversimplifying complex issues. Instead, using the guidance that comes from knowing and respecting the congregation, they are able to determine when and how they can invite the congregation into deeper waters of the faith.

CHAPTER 10

Help Us Get It Right

Chapter 8, "Talk about Everything," encourages clergy to preach on topics that might, at first thought, seem inappropriate or too "hot" to discuss from the pulpit. We present material indicating the respondents' readiness to hear about these issues from a faith perspective, which means with proper biblical and theological guidance. They look to their pastors and priests to provide that guidance.

In this chapter we listen to additional voices from the pews that ask their preachers for correction and direction in the respondents' thinking about and living out the Christian faith, especially when that implies some difficult adjustments. Although we have looked at how laity ask preachers to "Show How the Gospel Helps Us," the responses in this chapter push for an additional depth. We attempt here to allow the interweaving of ideas from various chapters to come through even more fully, for the inter-working of these suggestions from laity should result in a more fruitful time of preaching and more opportunities for congregations to grow deeper in the faith.

Requirements of the Christian Faith

The participants in the study often express a desire for sermons that help them individually and as congregations to understand the ongoing requirements of the Christian faith. When people suspect they are not living the religious life as fully as they believe they could, they lean forward in their pews, silently asking the preachers to "help us get it right."

In the pages that follow, we show that their requests for help are accompanied by a recognition that the sermon should not spoon-feed listeners, but requires personal reflection and often results in pain from stretching and growing in the faith. We also note the hesitance some clergy experience when considering difficult ideas. In addition, we cite some specific examples of times sermons helped people get it right.

This Is Important Stuff

As we move further into the research material, we are reminded time and again of how much the laity want worship to be valuable. People listen carefully to sermons, because they think of them as crucial nourishment for the religious life. They are willing to recall what they hear, to reflect on it through the week, and to experience the discomfort of stretching beyond their current faith place. Hear the seriousness with which this respondent listens to sermons. "I hang on to every scrap of information and knowledge that I can coming from my pastors, from anyone who preaches the Word of God. I hang on to that, and I use that to go back into the world and minister to people myself."

The preaching event needs to be an even more significant responsibility when we realize there are people who "hang on to every scrap" they can get from sermons and expect to be nourished by them through the week. This idea is repeated in the following responses:

> I take notes every Sunday, whatever minister is there. Every service I can, I always take notes, because I like to look back and reflect and meditate on what was said. I do. I get convicted. What I did XYZ days ago, I should not have done. Then I will correct. I'll make a correction and fix it. When you're trying to live a Christian life, these are just things that you do.

Another person agrees. "I sometimes reflect back on sermons; I reflect back on some scriptures, some things that will help me to maintain a level, a good Christian level with some of the knuckleheads I have to deal with on a day-to-day basis."

When people take preaching seriously, they want to hear new ideas; they want to learn new ways to get the faith right. They are willing for the sermon to stretch them. "It's good for you to go outside your level of comfort every now and then." And so, many are willing to hear whatever the preacher presents, trusting it will be beneficial to growing in the faith. Echoing ideas from the chapter on laity's willingness to hear about everything, one person articulates the belief that nothing is too explosive to preach about. "No. I think sex should be preached from the pulpit. I think money should be preached from the pulpit. I think racism should be preached against from the pulpit. If we're out of line with God, then I think it's the duty of the pastor to give us a word from the Lord that we need to get back into God's will."

The willingness to hear about difficult issues is not merely a willingness to hear Christianity's thoughts about issues, but a need to know God's perspective and will for making changes and living in the midst of these issues. The sermon is often seen as an essential tool for building a mature faith. One cannot hear one sermon and know the faith. It takes ongoing worship experiences as well as personal study and reflection to get deeper in the faith.

We remember listeners who want sermons to open up the Bible and then apply those lessons to today. A respondent in a small group interview expresses a desire to push even more. "This takes it a step further. Perhaps that's because I'd like to think a few steps ahead of where I was then." A little later in the interview, this same person clarifies the desire for those next steps to include the difficult areas of life. "I think a lot of times the things that preachers are afraid to talk about are the things that you need to talk about the most, because that's where the problems are."

The desire is to push beyond what Christians could or should think about a certain issue, to the question of how we are to change our lives to comply with those ideas. Laity want the sermon to invite them into the sometimes painful process of change. Of course, people do not want their every behavior dictated by the preacher. Their appeal is for the preacher to present new information and new ways of thinking about topics. They want to be challenged with new ideas that they then have to take time to think about, to put into practice. This person shows a preference for pastoral direction that depends on God's participation and personal will:

> I think authority in a sermon generally works best when it challenges me in a way that makes me want to make the decision myself, as opposed to saying, "You must do this." I think you can feel called out by the sermon. If you're teetering on that brink and saying, "Do I really have the time to do this?" "Do I really have the inclination?" "Am I going to make the devotion to take this next step in my life or do this?" You can hear a call in the sermon.

Another person agrees that the preacher is most effective when she or he offers new ideas about the faith. "Our minister challenges your ways of thinking about the scriptures that are being addressed at the time. I call it my old way of seeing about it. The sermon challenges that and causes you to think."

As noted above, in reporting how important some of our interviewees think preaching is, we are also presenting an interweaving of ideas of other chapters. Often this reflects the respondent's unconscious supposition that various parts of the preaching event are inseparable. As a person responds to one particular area of investigation, another area overlaps; and the respondent feels the need to comment on this other area as well. Other times, the interweaving of ideas is the result of interactions that occur in the small group interviews. One person puts forward responses and examples. Then others in the group develop or modify them.

Consider this example, which comes as one group discusses various types of sermons. The key remains the desire to receive something practical from the listening:

I don't have anything against emotional sermons, but it's clear that this sermon has an objective. It's well organized, and it's presented so that I can understand it. It is one that somewhere in the sermon what's being preached about is related to my everyday living and my striving to be a better Christian. I've been to sermons that I used to think were very good sermons, because everyone got up and hollered; but when I went away, the next day I couldn't remember anything at all from that sermon. I remember some things that happened, but not something that would impact on my life. I come to get something so when I go away I can use what I get.

Other small group interviews share the desire for sermons that make a difference in living. For instance, one person describes two different types of sermons, one preached in a friend's church, the other preached in the congregation in which the interviews are taking place. "I'm saying there's nothing wrong with feel-good messages, but there's nothing wrong with a feel-bad message either." After describing the setting of the friend's church, which has only "feel good" sermons, the person continues, "That's not church, in the sense that you've got to be careful of whose toes you're stepping on, because the Lord doesn't take the lead in that church. The preacher does to a degree; the clock does to a degree. But I'm hoping that the preacher at the church I choose to go to is doing what the Lord has led him or her to do, and I'll get a finger pointed at me a lot."

Preacher Hesitance

Interestingly, numerous laypersons express the desire for preachers to go ahead and "step on their toes" if it will help them mature in the faith. Still, quite a few of our interviews with ministers and priests in these same congregations uncovered a hesitance on the part of the clergy to do just that. Several preachers remind us that people do not speak with unanimity about wanting their toes stepped on. We acknowledge that some clergy have gotten into hot water, even dismissed, over their attempts to help the congregation "get it right"; but some of their parishioners are still claiming these ministers need to preach the Word nonetheless.

We reproduce two responses from preachers of different denominations: one urban congregation, the other rural; one quite relaxed in worship style, the other liturgical; one male pastor, and the other female. Both indicate reasons (some of which are good) for avoiding sermons that might step on toes or raise up issues that are too "hot."

The first preacher speaks with sensitivity, admitting: "There are times when I maybe wouldn't say what I'm convicted of, because it's a personal conviction, and I know that it's not held by a vast majority of the congregation. I don't think it's fair to throw it out in a sermon when you don't have a chance to discuss it." The preacher mentions a specific "hot topic" about which they may disagree, then continues:

> Not only is it dangerous to me as their pastor because it can shut down the relationship. We always have to be the pastor to all the people, so you have to be careful what you preach so that you can keep those communication doors open. The other thing is, I just don't see it's fair sometimes to throw out a one- or two-liner that may be misunderstood or that maybe someone wants to rebut, but they don't have a forum.

The minister of the other congregation begins by explaining the necessity of being oneself completely in the pulpit. "I find that in order to be an effective minister, I've got to be myself." Yet, when asked if there are times for holding back, for instance on certain topics, the minister strikes a chord that has a ring similar to the comments of the other preacher. "Even to this day, I think I don't want to criticize our local major employer for its monopolistic approach to business too much, because that could kill off my budget." However, the preacher goes on to discuss the importance of not trying to please everyone, concluding, "I think there's a great liberation once you find out that it's more important to be faithful in this work than it is to be successful, and it's impossible to please everybody. You become a lot better preacher and pastor."

These clergy want to be fully present in the pulpit, while keeping the doors of communication open with all parishioners and not wanting to suffer economic repercussions from sermons that step on toes. They are trying to find some middle ground–being themselves without alienating others. Some laity agree that the preacher's job is to speak a godly word, but would push the preacher to worry less about congregational toes.

Listeners need assistance from the pulpit to keep maturing in the faith, which means the preacher needs to speak some difficult words. "You [the preacher] can't hear God's word with baggage from people not liking you, what you're wearing, Sister So-and-so over here saying something. Then your job is not to be a minister, because you can't hear what God is saying to you. You can't deliver." To help the preacher, this respondent is willing to get personally involved. "I would just come right up and say, 'You know what? I think you need to de-baggage.'" Of course, most parishioners are not as straightforward to offer this kind of advice; and not all clergy would welcome it if they did.

Lay Willingness

Our respondents share various ideas that display their willingness to listen. Often they admit that trust is a central issue. Some sermon listeners indicate that their willingness to hear and put continuing effort into change depends on the level of trust in the preacher's own faith, intellect, and personhood, in which we can hear echoes of the need to know the preacher can "walk the walk."

Among other things, trust in the preacher comes from knowing that the preacher knows the congregation and is walking with them. "What I'm saying when we're talking about sermons, when you go with a sermon, know what your audience is. Know where your people are. Know what you need to do to move your congregation from here to here. When you get here, you can do things that if you did back here, you'd run them away."

The ability to trust the preacher is sometimes broken by how the sermon is presented, as this listener's response shows: "Some people's delivery made me doubt their sincerity. It would be someone who was just too perfect. When it's too packaged, it generally makes me suspicious." Note, the suspicion is not that the ideas are false, but that the preacher is. Another response gives an example of how a sermon might shut the communication doors and prevent a whole congregation's hearing a word intended to help get it right. "That minister could have gotten up and said, 'There are people like our sister here that ain't giving.' That probably would have hampered her from ever getting that message." Then the respondent adds that, in addition, such a message "turns off everybody else." This type of preaching hampers the hearing by hampering the ability to trust.

Sometimes trust is gained by the preacher's willingness to be open to hear what the congregation says about her or his sermons.

> Our Sunday school class for several summers had a talk back time after the service to say, "Okay, when you preached that, what did you mean about this?" I found those to be very helpful when we were doing those. You got a lot more out of the sermon when you had that talk back time where the minister relaxed and we could tell each other just what we thought.

If the minister trusts them enough to listen to their feedback, they can trust her or him to preach a sermon worth listening to. They are also willing to engage the sermon when the minister or priest treats them as real people. "I felt welcome. I was able to get into the choir immediately. There's a lot of stuff. There was room. A lot of churches you go to, you don't have room. You go, and you have to wait. But here: 'Get busy!' I like that. The first Sunday I came, the pastor let me sing. The pastor let me participate."

Laity are willing to receive even difficult messages when they sense the humanity of their preacher, as noted in this individual's response. "I like it to be a personal testimony as well to tell me the Word. Then how you apply it and what I need to do. I like for the Word to come back. Our preacher steps on my toes often, because it's like, 'Okay, that wasn't talking personally to me.' But then I see other people, too. I'd like for you to preach the Word that I can use it to better my life."

Although many persons seem willing to listen to almost anything when the preacher is trustworthy, we remember there are limits, as noted by the young person cited in chapter 9, who suggests that the male preacher needs to avoid instructing young women about postponing sex.

The willingness of, and the limits to, congregational listening are well described by one respondent who recognizes the importance of the sermon in the life of the congregation. "When we look for someone to call as minister, you look for someone whose preaching will pull people together. There are a lot of things you're looking for—someone who will not alienate the congregation, someone who manages the church well—but I think preaching is what we judge them on." The respondent adds an additional comment about the importance of ongoing growth resulting from the sermon: "I do look to be challenged. I don't want somebody to tell me what I knew last week and the week before. I want them to be a step ahead of me and hopefully bring me along with them."

Examples

Sometimes it is difficult for listeners to articulate how willing they are to hear a message from the pulpit that pushes them deeper into the Christian walk. Often they are better able to give an example of a sermon that facilitated such a change. We cite these examples, not for clergy to attempt to preach identical sermons, but to recognize the ongoing desire listeners have for help in increasing their faith and to share the promising news that preaching is making a difference in the lives of congregations around the country.

The first instance concerns the issue of financial support of the church, which is almost too thorny for some preachers to broach. The respondent has been asked about a sermon that caused a change in thinking. The response indicates the change is even more profound than merely thinking about money.

> Yes, it was about giving. That made me think very seriously about supporting the church and its work and about giving. I've heard a sermon that let me know that the churches need support. The preacher compared the church to other institutions like your home and your school. That it has needs that have to be supported. You have a pastor which has to be paid. In fact, we should have a budget. I just never thought of it that way. That sermon affected me very much in my life, in my church, and in my giving.

Another instance of a change comes from a small group interview, where the participants discuss the new priest's preaching, which often focuses on creating relationships between an individual and God, within the congregation as a whole, and even beyond.

INTERVIEWEE 1: For our previous pastor, the focus was Bible teaching. For our pastor now, the focus, as everybody agrees, is relationships. I think that as a result of that and the focus in a lot of our sermons, that our congregation has been more mindful of creating better relationships. I think before, even though the focus was Bible study, we still had a lot of problems going on, but now it seems as though the congregation has come together as a whole to make things better. It is better.

INTERVIEWEE 2: I think once the sermon goes to everybody and you think about when they were saying your relationships with God and with everybody else, I think it has made a difference. I mean you can only really attribute it to the sermon. The people are still the exact same people that have always been here. Right?

Preachers can take heart from the reports from many laypeople that the sermon is a significant influence in the life and shape of the congregation.

Laity Are Working Too

We wish it were not so, but wars happen in congregations. People have been known to fight over how often to have communion, who can be ordained, what type of music can be sung, what color of carpet to put in the balcony, who may speak from the pulpit, whether drums are appropriate in the sanctuary, and any number of other topics. Clergy and laity alike find parts of ecclesial life frustrating, even disheartening. Yet, laity keep coming back on Sundays to worship, because they believe what happens there is crucial to their faith. The faith is important to church people, and they are often willing to do serious work to deepen their individual faith and strengthen the bonds of the congregation. People look to their priests and ministers as they roll up their sleeves for the work, especially the assistance that comes from the pulpit. And, they are often willing to follow the preacher's lead.

Consider this person, who recognizes that changing and growing in the faith is not always easy:

> I personally don't always feel better after hearing everything, because I know I've done that, and I don't feel good about that. Or I've done something that I don't feel good about what I've done, but sometimes the sermon just brings that out and makes me aware of it. So to me, that's growth. That's good because I should be aware of what I'm doing or not doing or could be doing better.

Another person opens up an experience in which it was only in conversation with a family member after worship that the full impact of the sermon struck home. The after-worship conversation moved around to the sermon, and the interviewee admits there was "attitude" in the feelings and expressions made about it. A family member pointed out that this "attitude" arose because the person had been "convicted," saying, "You know that you are not right about this topic." The person reporting the incident goes on to admit:

> It made me open my eyes and just really look and start thinking. I didn't go there with the right attitude. I was being convicted, and it wasn't the preacher preaching it. It was me feeling that the conviction was coming from above. So I felt like, "Yes, I'm not doing what God wants me to do." Only after we talked about it, then it came to me; and I recognized what was happening. It was something in the sermon that I needed to do to adjust myself and my attitude toward what was being preached that day.

The person concludes with the recognition, "As a member, sometimes you don't like to hear what the minister is saying."

Interestingly, such reports are often offered with an intense sense of appreciation for the various forces at work provoking the changes, as difficult as they are. Reporting on a congregational controversy, one listener confides: "Well, at least we had it out. It wasn't something that we didn't talk about and didn't happen, because it did; and it was huge. There were parts of it where the preacher asked us to stand up if we were angry and things like that...Sometimes I think we need to be pushed to sort out feelings."

Two final comments from individuals show appreciation for the complicated work sermons do: "I always come in to receive what God has said. Then I apply it to my life. I stop something. It's like, 'Okay, you can't continue to do this. You're going to hear my word.' So I apply it to my life. So it makes a change. I change."

And finally, this person sums up the opinion of many respondents:

> What preaching does that nothing else does? I think it probably challenges you more than any other element does. I think we also look at preaching to bring us back to the Bible. I think that you can come for the special things, and you can come for the service projects, and you feel good about doing those; but something has to connect it to why you're doing it. I think the sermon is generally the glue that does that.

Talk Loud Enough So We Can Hear

The last question asked in most of our interviews is, "If you had one or two things you could tell preachers that would help them turn you on when you are listening to a sermon, what would they be?" Among the most common recommendations are variations on (a) to "work on your delivery and make that part of the message interesting," and (b) to develop content that applies to real life. Listeners often use the language of "delivery" to refer to the physical presence of the preacher in the pulpit. Many, however, understand that in the moment of preaching the minister does not simply "deliver" the sermon with the same relationship to the content that the postal carrier has to parcel post. The preacher *embodies* the sermon. As one of the interviewees says, "You can't just separate the message from the manner in which it is given."[1]

The interviewees elaborate on several traits of embodiment. Recognizing that these things work together with one another in a gestalt with the content of the message, we lift up the following perspectives: being able to hear, variety in the use of the voice, energy and conviction, eye contact, gestures and body language, movement out of the pulpit, annoying mannerisms, and the preacher's pulpit presence being consistent with the preacher's personality.

The chapter title is taken from an interviewee who sometimes has difficulty hearing the preacher and whose admonition reminds us that the preacher cannot simply take embodiment for granted but needs to be intentional in seeing that these elements are present.

Despite the enthusiasm for lively embodiment that is present in many interviews, we do need to acknowledge that some listeners say that embodiment is inconsequential. "I don't care [about embodiment]. I really don't care. I think it's where you are spiritually. I don't go to worship because of their skill. Personally it doesn't matter."

The Congregation Needs to Hear

Many persons in this study make the very basic point that they need to be able to hear the sermon. As one says, "When you can't hear, everything else can go by the wayside." Other listeners similarly lament the inability to hear. "If you can't hear, sometimes you fill in the blanks. You hear some things you want to hear. Being able to hear is a huge issue for me."

With respect to being able to hear, some listeners urge preachers to make sure that the public address system is working, and that they know how to use it. One interviewee remembers an occasion when "the preacher was backing away from the mike and stuff. I couldn't hear, so I fell asleep. It's like sometimes, 'Eh? Eh?' And you don't know what they're saying. You don't get it."

Another person comments, "At times, when the microphones don't work, that's distracting. When they have to look back at the corner and say, 'Am I on?'" Insofar as possible, preachers should check the public address system before the service to determine that it is working and that they know how to use it.

Variety and Inflection in the Voice

A significant number of listeners stress that the preacher needs to pronounce the words of the sermon so that people can understand them. Such hearers are engaged by vocal variety that is consistent with the content of the sermon, as well as by preachers who skillfully use pauses in their sermons.

Preachers need to enunciate clearly and to speak at a speed that makes it easy for people to follow the sermon. "It's where someone comes in and mutters something we can't understand that bothers me," one contributor notes.

Another person says more firmly, "The minister may very well have something superb, but I have a little hearing problem anyway. So if you use poor diction, I'm in real trouble."

With regard to the use of the voice, a preacher's having a monotone quality is perhaps the largest single complaint of the body of people interviewed for this research. Here are comments whose themes are reproduced in many others:

"Monotone, just yada, yada, yada. Those lose my attention and put me to sleep."

"If they're just standing up there and reading everything off in monotone, I can hardly stay awake. You've wasted a sermon."

The positive suggestion that emerges from this concern is that the preacher can enhance the experience of the sermon for the congregation by manifesting variety in the use of the voice. "The preacher knows how to change the voice to make it more meaningful to everyone listening. This preacher does not continue with the same tone throughout the whole sermon or the whole service."

Some congregants make a point of commending preachers who not only speak with vocal variety but who make sure their voice tones are consistent with the content of the message.

> I like people who are more up and down, depending on what they're saying. If there's excitement, they have passion and they get excited. Then they say it, and they back off. I think using the dramatics of soft is very good. Soft is very powerful to me. Just knowing when to engage in the passion and the loud and when to back off. Where the passion needs to be, and when the humility needs to be there, or when being vulnerable needs to be there.

We receive similar insights from other persons in the study sample. "The tone in the sermon needs to coordinate with what the preacher is saying. The preacher gets emotional and can get excited. The preacher can get sad, have anger in the voice, but it goes with the message. That makes it seem more sincere. It's not just delivery of words on the paper." The sermon gains integrity between content and delivery when the tone of voice is aligned with the content of the message.

As noted previously, quite a number of respondents call attention to the pause and silence in the sermon as moments that draw them deeper into the message. "Use silence a lot," says one parishioner, meaning that it lets the person ponder the preacher's point.

Another says similarly, "I like our minister's preaching style. This preacher knows how to pause and give emphasis to something."

However, a preacher needs to be careful not to soften the voice so much that it is lost on the congregation.

> Our minister gets real loud and then real soft. The preacher gets real soft and I can't hear. Unfortunately, this preacher usually makes the important point while whispering. I get in the front, but still can't hear. It's good that it gets your attention—the change of volume—but it's not good for those of us who are older and can't hear well.

Another hearer reports a similar experience. "We had a preacher here that we just loved. This person would preach, then when getting ready to make the point or summarize, would just drop the head. People were constantly saying to me, 'We can't hear the preacher. We can't hear it.'"

Eye Contact

Almost as many interviewees speak about the importance of eye contact as mention the importance of being able to hear. Eye contact, for many of these folk, establishes a sense of being in touch with another human being. "You need a personal contact. You need eye-to-eye contact so you can get a feel along with what they're saying. You can talk and speak very well, but you need direct eye contact that gives you a presence with the congregation or another individual."

Indeed, another person agrees:

> If we can't see them, we really don't know how real they are and how real the message is to them. It's like somebody just sitting there and talking. You get this recording of someone and say, "Evaluate it." Well, you can't really evaluate it just based upon words. You've got to see the person to see if they're really filled up with what they're saying.

These interviewees perceive eye contact as a matter of human-to-human connection.

Judging by the number of listeners in the study who object to the preacher reading the sermon, a fair percentage of preachers must be doing just that. Several interviewees said, simply, "Don't read to us."

No one in the study complains about the preacher using notes as long as the preacher speaks the sermon and does not obviously read it. "A good speaker can use notes without appearing to use notes. You can use notes and speak as though you don't have notes, which to me makes a difference."

Another person says approvingly, "The pastor does not read the sermons. The pastor may have sixteen pages but doesn't read them. The pastor uses them for notes, more or less."

Seeing the face is important to some listeners. "With my hearing, I need to see the face, and that helps me focus on the delivery."

Another person has the personal insight that "I'm a visual person. We listen down here [in the fellowship hall preparing for the coffee hour after worship] all the time, but it is more powerful for me to be front and center. I've got to see." For still others, being able to see the face is a part of the human connection. "Seeing the face helps you see that a live person is talking. It helps you to connect." Another says, "I'm sensitive to facial expressions. I want to see the face." Not reading allows the preacher to look fully at the congregation so that they can see the preacher's face.

The clergy in the congregations in the study were also interviewed. Although this is not the place for comparative analyses of preachers and their congregations, we do note responses from a pastor and a layperson who preaches occasionally, who both intentionally avoid making eye contact with the congregation. The layperson who preaches from time to time says, "I don't stare at one person. I find a blind spot on the wall, and I stand there with my eyes big. I'll rock my head all night, but I never leave that one mark on the wall, to never single any one person out." The full-time preacher reflects,

> For the most part, I certainly don't intentionally make eye contact with anybody, because first of all I feel that, for the same reason that after a marriage ceremony I don't go to the bedroom and watch the couple have sex together. Preaching is such a personal, an intensely personal, experience that I feel that it's an invasion of their privacy for me to make eye contact, so I don't for the most part make eye contact.

This preacher does not read the sermon. This minister preaches without notes but looks at the floor, over the heads of the congregation, and at a chapel adjoining the sanctuary. While these two preachers perceive this behavior as respecting the privacy of the congregation, the people in their congregations, in interview after interview, report that they *want* eye contact.

Asked about some physical things their preachers could do to help increase listeners' attention, an interviewee in one of the congregations says, "Well, sure. Eye contact can. That's not one of our minister's strengths." In response to the same question, another communicant in the same congregation speaks of physical things that the preacher does.

> I know I don't like a lot of hand movement, so I think that could be a negative. Things that do keep my attention, though. Looking out in the crowd and maybe making eye contact with you. Some preachers I know preach just off the page and read it, but when they look at the crowd and make the eye contact, I think it holds me more accountable to pay attention.

Asked to enumerate one or two things that the congregant would like to tell preachers, a member of the same church said, "First thing, I suppose, would be, 'Look at me,' because if you're not looking at me and you're looking someplace else, if you're not looking out at us but looking off into the distance, there's no feeling that I have to look back at you." Furthermore, according to this respondent, avoiding the congregation deprives the preacher of an important opportunity to assess the impact of the sermon and make adjustments along the way to give the listening community a greater opportunity to engage the message. "If you're looking out at the congregation, 'How many people are watching me, and how many people are off doing something else?' I think storytellers and stand-up comics are in exactly the same kind of business, that they have to be able to read the audience and to know whether the audience is with them or not." To be sure, preachers have a different relationship with the listeners than storytellers and stand-up comics but preachers can still learn about the importance of eye contact from them.

Energy and Conviction

A number of participants in our study indicate they are likely to engage with preachers who speak with energy and conviction, whereas they tend to withdraw from sermons that lack conviction. "If the person is enthusiastic about preaching and trying to teach you what they know, and they can get that enthusiasm across on Sunday morning, that helps me more than anything." Furthermore, "you need to feel what you're talking about because when you feel it, whether or not I'm going to agree with it or not, at least I know that's where you are with it. That it's real for you at that point."

Other hearers speak specifically of responding positively not just to the preacher's enthusiasm and energy, but to the feeling of passion.

> Emotion makes a difference for me. Maybe it's one of the few things that I really like about some old-fashioned types of sermons—what is sometimes called "fire and brimstone," but I don't mean it as the sort of "You are damned if you don't" kind of passion, but just the passion that can be available in some presentations of material. That's the message that I remember or that really makes a difference for me. It actually starts to make me think differently when someone's really got a vibrancy.

When speaking of passion, several listeners clearly have in mind not just emotionalism but passion as a feeling that arises from deep within the preacher.

> I think it's necessary that the preacher try to reach some kind of basic emotion in people. You recall that everybody [in this group] who earlier talked about a sermon that they recall or that really touched them, it was something personal and emotional. I don't go for it just being all emotional. There are some churches where it's just showing raw emotions where that's all that's going on. That's not what I'm talking about. But there definitely needs to be an emotional connection. The pulpit presence is a big issue in how well the sermon comes across. I had a friend, a very dear friend, a wonderful minister and all of that, but was the worst speaker I had ever heard. The content was solid and good, but this preacher was terrible. All I could think about was, "Oh, my friend, this is awful." That person lost you, because I think the person in the pulpit has to be passionate.

Passion is not a substitute for thought, but without passion, the thought of the sermon is sometimes like seed that lands on dry soil.

Gestures and Body Language

A fair sample of interviewees say they respond positively to preachers who bring the sermon to life with gestures and whose body language in the pulpit is consistent with the message and its feeling. For example, an interviewee favorably speaks of a preacher from a previous congregation who had an effective embodiment. "That preacher was really animated–had a lot of movement."

Another member of the study population says their preacher has "inflection, and uses the hands a lot." A member of a small group asks, "Does it add or take away when somebody is gesturing? I'm from the East Coast, so I talk with my hands." Other people respond to the question, "It can add." "It can help."

Gestures, like the use of the voice and passion, are more than technique. Gestures are a part of a preacher's language. We hear this concern in an interviewee's response to a question about qualities of embodiment that can interfere with paying attention to the sermon.

INTERVIEWEE: Gestures that are not choreographed. I guess we've all seen those. Effective delivery, I think, goes back toward if they're trying to make a show of the sermon, or are they honestly giving me their opinion? Gestures are very appropriate at times. I think that's the key determination on how we view the overall presentation as very sincere and appropriate as opposed to show and their agenda.

INTERVIEWER: So some gestures could stand in the way.

INTERVIEWEE: Yes. When they don't fit.

A person trained in counseling who was in the interview group says, "Their body language speaks. In my profession you're taught to watch the body language because a person can tell you one thing and be hiding from you. The preacher's body language does mean a lot in their delivery. 'Your body was speaking so loud, I couldn't hear what you were saying.'" For such folk who sit in the pew week after week, the way the preacher's expression comes through the body is a measure of the authenticity of the sermon.

Preaching outside the Pulpit

The survey questions did not include one that specifically asked how the listeners respond to the preacher's leaving the pulpit and delivering the sermon from the chancel steps or even the floor of the congregation. However, this phenomenon is increasing, and a number of people volunteered that they feel engaged by this phenomenon.[2] Two ministers in a congregation did a dialogue sermon. "They stood in front, right down on the floor. They didn't share the pulpit, and they had notebooks or something, and they both preached. They took turns. It was something different and caught our attention." A fuller statement from another interviewee makes a similar point.

When the pastor comes around to the front of the podium, I always sit up just a little bit straighter because I know whatever the preacher is going to say is going to be just a little more important. The preacher is stressing something by coming out from behind that podium. Sometimes the preacher comes down the steps on our level, and I'm thinking, "This is going to be really big. Whatever the preacher is going to say now, the preacher really wants us to grasp."

These listeners are attracted to the sermon given from the floor, at least in part, because it is unusual. Other listeners to whom such occurrences are more regular also warm to it. "This pastor would go out into the congregation and the whole time just walk around while preaching. You're not going to see too many people falling asleep when you do that. What's that preacher doing down here?"

As we said, however, not everyone appreciates the preacher leaving the pulpit. "That just turns me off to them, parading around and yelling and carrying on. That delivery I don't really care for. But I don't want them to read the sermon, either.

Avoid Distracting Mannerisms

Several listeners in our project say that preachers sometimes manifest mannerisms in the pulpit that distract them. Preachers unconsciously repeat such mannerisms with the effect that listeners may begin to pay more attention to the mannerism than to the content of the sermon. For example, one listener began to count the number of times a pastor used an expression during a sermon. "I had a minister that fifteen times during the sermon would say, 'If you will.' So I was never sure whether to believe that minister or not, because it didn't sound like the minister was sure."

While ministers need to determine mannerisms that their own congregations may find distracting, here are some that come up in the interviews. "I was in the car one time with a bunch of tapes from a minister that I happen to really like, but this minister constantly says, 'Now, listen. Now, listen. Now, listen.'" This respondent turned off the tape. Another says, "I do not like slangy delivery," that is, the use of too much slang in the sermon. In the midst of describing embodiment that is engaging, another hearer says, "There's no 'Uh,' none of that." Still another says, "If I had my way, I would not let a preacher get in the pulpit and say, 'Mmmmm-mmmmm. Mmmmmmmmm.' I can't take that. It takes them I don't know how long to say two or three words because it's 'Mmmmm.'" The minister clicking the tongue is another example of a mannerism that some parishioners find annoying. Other "ministers have a trait in which they 'Uhhhhhhh,' breathe in. I can't stand it. It's like I'm choking when they do."

Different people find different things annoying. There may be people in the same congregations who like the mannerisms we report as distracting (although no one in any of the interviews in the same congregations took issue with any of the criticisms that other parishioners voiced). In any event, the preacher needs to be brave enough to ask trusted members of the congregation for feedback about mannerisms.

Get Help If Needed

Several parishioners suggest that preachers seek help in improving their embodiment. One says, for instance,

> Enroll in Toastmasters. Or I don't know if there are seminars. But a weekly, nonthreatening support group for many pastors to help them with public speaking, not on the message but on their delivery, will go a long way, I think, in improving the quality of many, many churches. The preacher can't just stand up there and expect to be inspired, and the Word of God is going to come out and be delivered.

In one congregation in the study sample, a minister meets regularly with a speech teacher who is in the congregation to receive feedback concerning this preacher's embodiment.

Presence in the Pulpit Consistent with Presence Elsewhere

In chapter 2, we comment on the importance of ministerial integrity—"walking the walk" or "practicing what you preach." Here we call attention to a related dimension of integrity: using the voice and the body in the pulpit in ways that are consistent with the way the preacher speaks and moves in everyday life. One congregant recounts, "I think it's important that preachers stay within their personalities." Another listener commends, "Be aware of your own strengths and weaknesses, and do not try to be someone else. That is always the earmark of a great preacher—being yourself." We hear the importance of this perspective underlined in the follow exchange.

INTERVIEWER: Would you describe for me a preacher whose physical presence in the pulpit was really good, whose delivery was engaging?

INTERVIEWEE: There's a fine line on that one, because it can be both what you like and what you dislike. Our minister is very, very good about engaging people, I think, by use of hand expressions and intonation of voice. Many times it's very, very effective, but there have been a few times when it felt like the preacher was just struggling to pull people in. The gestures and voice intonations were not quite whiny, but more, "Please, please, please," kind of thing as opposed to an invitation. It was begging versus an invitation.

INTERVIEWER: Is there a way for a preacher to know when they've crossed the line?

INTERVIEWEE: Part of it is a sense that they have. Part of it I believe you can see by looking in the faces of the congregation.

The interviewee makes a response that ties together the themes of this chapter. With respect to embodiment, the preacher is not simply a technician of the voice, gestures, and where to stand. Preachers need to be who they are both in and out of the pulpit, and to be able to engage in pastoral listening during the sermon itself and to adjust the sermon where needed.

CHAPTER 12

Don't Forget to Put in Your Teeth

An interviewer asks an older participant in the study, "Can you think of a time when you could not hear a preacher?" The interviewee replies, "Yes. You can never understand preachers who don't have their teeth in." The congregation had, indeed, heard a sermon from a preacher who left the false teeth at home with the consequence that the people had great difficulty understanding the message. As the interviewee notes, "That Sunday, let's just say, we left thinking, 'Okay, yes, I *think* we've been to church today.'"

Putting in one's teeth serves in this chapter as a symbol of simple but fundamental things that preachers can do to facilitate communication. When preachers forget these things, a good many listeners report that they do not tune into the sermon as well as when these qualities are present. We highlight the following matters that interviewees mention most frequently: knowing the congregation, talking about things that are close to your heart, preparing properly, speaking in language that people can understand, using variety in preaching style, using humor, maintaining a positive tone, not letting your ego overwhelm the sermon, being patient with the fact that people listen differently, and taking heart from the fact that many of the effects of preaching are cumulative.

Know the Congregation

A significant number of congregants in the study insist that the preacher needs to know the congregation.[1] Several listeners flatly say exactly that: "A minister needs to know the congregation." Such hearers most engage a sermon when they perceive that it is addressed to them in their particularity, while they tend to disregard messages that seem to be generic.

A key is for the preacher to include material in the sermon that resonates with the real-life experience of the listening community. "In the sermons, many times, I look at my spouse. 'Was the preacher in the kitchen last night when we were talking about this?'" Another respondent speaks similarly. "You think, 'Oh my gosh, there have been spies looking in our window.'" In connection with a particular sermon, an interviewee relates, "My spouse and I are both sitting there wiping our eyes. It was like, 'The preacher knows about this,' but the preacher didn't really know."

Knowing the congregation can help the preacher shape the sermon so that the congregation can engage it in an optimum way. "A minister needs to know the congregation. You have to look at your flock and see what your flock is able to handle, so we can continue to grow."

Under such conditions, reactions like the following are commonplace. "Our pastor can take the scripture, typically lessons for the day, and make them real in my life. It sounds like the pastor is talking directly to me. I heard somebody else say that to the preacher last Sunday. 'That sermon— you were talking directly to me.' You just hear that a lot around here." Another person says, "I don't know if the preacher gets on a bicycle or drives around the city in the car, or reads the newspapers, but the preacher is always able to bring it home where we live."

Talk about Things Close to Your Heart

A great number of parishioners with whom we spoke say that their interest in a sermon is often engaged when they sense that preachers are talking about things that are close to the preachers' hearts. As we note in the preceding chapter, a number of people listen for the preacher's passion for the topic of the sermon. On the other side, these parishioners report that they can often tell when the preacher is speaking about something in which the preacher has little interest and that they tend not to care about the sermon if the preacher seems not to care.

An interviewee expresses this concern very simply: "Preachers need to be coming from the heart and from their mind and be honest about what they're talking about. No fake stories and fake jokes they've gotten out of a book."

Some listeners report that they can tell when the sermon is not close to the preacher, as we notice in the following exchange. The interviewer asks a small group about sermons that did not interest them or left them cold.

INTERVIEWEE 1: When you sense that something is being held back, either for political reasons or because the audience won't receive it well. That's filtering. You can tell when somebody's filtering information or filtering some belief. You can tell they're holding it back.

INTERVIEWEE 2: Yes. A few years ago, there was something that came down from the [denominational governing body] in the summer. You could tell it was a topic the pastor had to preach on. The pastor was not a happy camper. It was not the best sermon, and it was mercifully brief.

INTERVIEWEE 3: It was almost one of those where you had, "Okay. I got my checkmark. It's done."

Preachers might ask, "Do I care enough about a particular topic to preach well on it?" When the preacher cares, the people tend to care.

Prepare

In chapter 6, "Keep It Short," we stress the importance of the preacher's preparing the sermon. As one listener says, "When you're up there and you're not prepared, it just makes me sick, and I think, 'What's the use in me being here?'"

Other interviewees make two suggestions to help ministers with sermon preparation. The first is that preachers should use a feed-forward group, that is, people who meet with the preacher while the sermon is being prepared and reflect with the preacher on how the biblical text intersects with their everyday experience.[2] In a variation, one of the ministers in our study sample has a group of people who help with researching the sermon. These people actually read books and articles and give relevant data to the preacher. Upon learning more about this process while being interviewed for this study, a parishioner who had not previously served as a ministerial research assistant said, "I'll call the preacher." This person wants to be a part of the research team.

The second suggestion is that ministers focus on preaching and get other people in the congregation to take responsibility for other aspects of leadership that do not require the pastoral hand. Someone interviewed for the study notices that in some churches "the preacher comes in and turns the lights on, gets communion ready, does bulletin, does the softball team." The listener admonishes the preacher to "get to the point where you teach the word. You delegate. No matter how small a church is, get somebody else to do these things, so you can spend more time studying." Another person in another congregation reinforces this point. "What hurts the church is a bad preacher with good administration tasks, because you can always pass the administration skills to someone else."

Speak in Language People Can Understand

One of the most insistent strains in listener comments is also one of the simplest: The preacher needs to speak in language that the people can understand. The congregation tends to drift out of the world of the sermon when the person in the pulpit uses words that the congregation does not know. A fair number of preachers, evidently, use words from the Bible or from the technical language of theology that are unfamiliar and neglect to help the congregation learn the meaning of those words.

One hearer reports frustration "when they start preaching and it's over everyone's head. They're using a lot of different terms and big words. They have to explain it to me." A member of a congregation that sometimes has a seminary student on the staff, says, "The sermon is sometimes not much in terminology that we even understand. They're preaching above our heads. They've lost us. They're preaching probably what they've heard in school that week, but they don't break it down for us." Still another listener puts this concern into a principle that every preacher can use. "Keep the sermon on our level."

Other interviewees appreciate pastors helping them understand the language of the sermon.

> I like when a minister is talking and can relate it to something personal. The minister is talking about biblical words that were written so long ago that sometimes it's hard to relate. I like for the ministers to take the biblical word, state it, and then rephrase it so that it has meaning for us.

A member of an urban congregation reminds us that "what people can understand" is contextual. "Some of these people come right off the street. The preacher has to stay within the limits of the city because that's the way they talk on the street, and that's probably the only way to reach some of them."

Reprising the earlier consideration of preparation and bringing it into dialogue with speaking so that everyone can understand, one listener says, "I think if you're going to preach on any subject, you have to have research. Research your message and make it so that everybody can understand what you're saying."

Variety in Preaching Style

Several people interviewed in the project indicate that they like occasional variety in the preaching style. A change in approach raises listener interest, as comes out in the following response to the question of what people find engaging. "Using a variety, not being predictable." Another person from the same congregation says, "Even though the person has been a minister for a long time, it's good for the minister to surprise us once in a while, not have the same predictable sermon over and over again."

Occasionally listeners take another step to suggest that variety is good for the preacher as well as for the congregation.

> I think maybe preachers need to take a chance. They need to step out of the box. They need to maybe get out of their comfort zone just a little bit. With anything, you get into a habit of doing

something the same way all the time everyday that you do it. Maybe you get a little bored with what you're doing. But if you take a chance and step out of the box and do something different, I think people are going to sit up and take notice a little bit more.

The energy created in the preacher by a change is contagious to the congregation.

In the early stages of the project, some of the project team members were surprised that many interviewees could not remember sermons in detail. They could remember moments from sermons—not whole sermons, but moments—such as illustrations, particular theological insights, even titles. In part, this phenomenon may result from the artificiality of the interview situation.

However, quite a few people are able to remember two kinds of sermons. For one, they recollect messages that were important to them at important life junctures—when they were confused, lost, or in pain either personally or socially. For example, one parishioner recalls such an occasion.

I remember a particular sermon which spoke to dealing with the stresses of seemingly not having enough time to do everything that you need to do and how we choose to prioritize or not prioritize or whatever, and about the presence or absence of a spiritual component in all of that. I think that the reason that it comes to mind is, again, that it precipitated so much discussion afterwards both between my spouse and myself, but also with other people. We stayed in the sanctuary and didn't go to Sunday school, a group of us sitting in the pews talking about it.

In the context of the full interview, it is clear that this listener—a high-powered urban professional—is on the go all the time, with multiple vocational, volunteer, and family activities. The content of the sermon intersected with an important concern at the heart of this listener's life, and, we surmise, with the lives of the other men and women who stayed in the sanctuary talking about the sermon.

The other kind of sermon they remember are those whose format is out of the ordinary. For example, a small number of listeners mention responding very favorably to sermons in which the preacher takes on the persona of a Biblical character. The reader will remember the listener quoted on page 41, who appreciated the preacher's speaking as an Old Testament prophet.[3] Members of another congregation remember a sermon in which the preacher dressed up like a baseball player and spoke from the aisle, comparing the life of faith to participation on an athletic team.

Occasionally, congregants raise cautions. "Creativity is good, but don't let it drive the whole process so that you're trying to entertain every week." While "a lot of people these days want to be entertained, that's not the reason we come to church."

A Little Humor Goes a Long Way

The presence of humor in the sermon draws a positive response from nearly everyone in the sample group who mentions it. One person says, "I think humor is a big help for a minister. Now I don't just mean the whole thing is joke, joke, joke, but a pastor can have a way of relating a joke to the point of the sermon." Often, humor helps establish identification, as the following remark indicates:

> I think the important thing is to use some story, and the more related that story would be to your audience, whether it's something you tell about yourself, or some friend that is easily identified, or some situation that you use to illustrate. If you can perhaps bring a little humor to the effort, I think that's good, too. Just make it personal, and that's one way of doing it.

A little self-exposing humor on the pastor's part can say, "I empathize with how you live." Another participant in the interviews says, "It's real easy to drift off, but then they have a little humor that brings you back and kind of makes you chuckle and think about it."

However, listeners raise cautions regarding the use of humor. When humor is not germane to the content of the sermon, it actually diverts listener attention.

> When one of our ministers first came, that preacher would get you right to the point, where you needed to be convicted or challenged or whatever. It made the preacher nervous, and the preacher would tell a joke. It would be funny, but it would lose everyone just like that.

Humor needs to coordinate with the direction of the sermon.

Some auditors also raise a caution against the use of joke books and similar sources of humor. One person says,

> So many of the stories I've heard in the past seem so artificial, seem to be made up to get to the point that is in the last paragraph of the sermon. That turns me off. A book of stories on the shelf somewhere. You pick up the book, 'Okay, I'm going to introduce the sermon with this story.' It's supposed to apply to us, but it doesn't. Or a joke book—that's even worse."

The best humor is that which preachers discover in the course of living.

Positive Tone

In our interviews, a great number of churchgoers expressed a preference for sermons that have a positive tone. As we point out in chapter 10, "Help Us Get It Right," most of the people who made suggestions on this point indicate they do want to know what they do wrong and to take responsibility for it. But they also hope the sermon will take the next step to naming good news regarding how God is present and active to help them become better people and the world to become a better place. They often use terms such as "assurance," "uplifting," and "inspirational" to describe sermons with this characteristic.

Several listeners make comments like, "The number one thing I like about the sermon is for it to be positive. Not just fear: 'If you don't do what I tell you to do, you're going to burn in hell.' I really like the positive aspect of the message." This listener acknowledges the need for the congregation to face its complicity in sin, "But if I'm going to be challenged, I need a motivation that's positive and not fear."

Such listeners often tune out preachers whom they perceive as continuously negative because such sermons are inconsistent with the divine purposes. "The sermons that turn me off are the ones that the pastor gets up before the congregation and starts to really downgrade people. That's not what God is about. God is about lifting people up."

When queried as to what would be energizing when hearing a sermon, one listener says, "To be truthful and to be up about it, because you can't make me do what is right if you are down and depressed about it." This person listens for a positive quality even in sermons about hard topics such as tithing, adultery, or death. Yes, the preacher should acknowledge the full array of difficulties and feelings that accompany such experiences, but the sermon should help the congregation make its way through them.

Don't Let Your Ego Overwhelm the Sermon

Only a few people mentioned the phenomenon of preachers making themselves the center of the sermon, but it comes into the transcripts of those interviews with considerable force. Interviewees perceive these preachers as not simply speaking out of their own experience (as we discuss in chapters 3 and 8), but as using the pulpit in ways that serve the preacher's own ego or even promote the preacher's personal gain.

A listener illustrates this phenomenon. "I've been in churches where the minister sits up there and it's almost a 'you shall bow to me' situation. This minister was very regal, very powerful. The minister was the central focal point and would never show any vulnerability."

Another listener reports a wider conversation in a congregation along this line. "I actually heard people talking about feeling offended that there was some self-laudatory stuff going on within the sermon. That's hard to listen to from the pulpit." In a similar vein, another says, "If the pastor is very arrogant and sitting up there with all this gold and gaudy look, that would make me think, 'Hmmmm. Is this person coming with the Word of God or just trying to sell something?'"

Be Patient When Different Listeners Hear Different Things

Preachers are sometimes perplexed and frustrated by the fact that different listeners hear different things in the same message. Listeners themselves, however, report that this phenomenon is not surprising. One says, "People really do have different attitudes about sermons." Another indicates, "Everybody in a congregation of a hundred people listening to the sermon—you can have a hundred different interpretations of what's being said."

Another person with whom we spoke explains that personal and social locations often impact how the listener receives the message.

> I think if the preacher hits me on the right Sunday, I'm a pretty good listener. It's not always the pastor. It's the kind of week you had, what you're reflecting on in your life as you sit in the pew. Sometimes the sermon can touch that part of your life. Other times you're still worrying about it while you're sitting there on a Sunday morning. It could be a variety of things way beyond a pastor's control that the listener is just not going to hear that Sunday.

No amount of rhetorical finesse can give the preacher control over congregational receptivity. Nevertheless, a participant in the study reminds us that the pastoral vocation includes preparing sermons so that people have a good chance to get the message.

> I don't think a preacher can always connect with everybody, but I think you can always structure what you're trying to say to capture a larger percentage than a smaller percentage. You have to structure it so that most people can get something of what you're saying.

A well-prepared sermon gives the congregation an opportunity to welcome its contents when they are at a point in life to receive it.

Be Encouraged by the Cumulative Effects of Preaching

In gatherings of clergy, we frequently hear hard-working, sincere ministers recount a particular sermon, but then lament, "I just can't tell that it had any effect." The people in our study who mentioned this topic urge the preacher not to be discouraged. While some listeners say they are occasionally directly affected by a particular sermon, more of the time the effects of preaching are cumulative. Even when they cannot remember specific sermons, they are aware that over time, preaching has touched their thoughts, feelings, and actions.

One listener says, "I can't really put my finger on one sermon that, when I walked out the door, I said, 'This is going to affect me. I'm a changed person right now.' I think it's kind of a progression." Another says, similarly, "Individual sermons don't tend to stick out. Maybe that's a reflection on me more than anything else. But sermons affect me by their general trends."

The following remark resonates similarly. "There probably have been a couple of sermons that you walked out of there and said you had this enlightenment, this 'Wow!' But I really think it's mostly an accumulation. It's an evolution." Another interviewee uses a very similar expression in making the same point, "I think that the sermons are part of the journey in most cases for me. So there's not that many 'Wow' moments. There don't have to be if they help me grow."

Still another interview reinforces this idea:

> I don't expect every sermon every week to be stunning. A lot of times sermons grow on you. You come to understand a person's way of preaching. They can have a power over a period of weeks that is maybe not stunning the first time. You look at the pattern that they develop over time. Maybe partly, we learn to hear what this particular preacher has to say.

The effects of sermons often accumulate much like water slowly dripping from the faucet into a bowl in the kitchen sink at night. You might not notice more than a little dampness right after supper and just a little pool at bedtime, but by morning, the water overflows.

The research team surmised correctly that we could discover the significance of preaching by asking people to reflect on what the church would be like without it. An interchange in a small group summarizes a view of preaching held in common by the great majority of persons who spoke with our study team. An interviewer asks the question, "What would be missing if there were no sermon?"

INTERVIEWEE 1: Without the sermon? That's the heart. That's the heart of the worship.
INTERVIEWEE 2: Like somebody stealing the engine out of your car.
INTERVIEWEE 3: Yes. It's just like a body with no heart. You can't beat. It's the pulse. It's the life.
INTERVIEWEE 4: It's what you want to take with you throughout the week.
INTERVIEWEE 5: Throughout your life.
INTERVIEWEE 6: Amen.

Surely, then, the task of preaching deserves our most creative, focused, faithful, and passionate effort.

Putting the Advice to Work

Sample Sermons

The interviews on which this book rests do not produce a singular theory of preaching. They suggest, rather, that many different ingredients of preaching can serve as effective communication channels for the gospel. In every case, however, the approach for a particular sermon must be theologically meaningful, in touch with the context in which the preaching takes place, consistent with the person of the preacher, and embodied with life and vitality. The twelve commonly held perspectives identified in this volume can serve the gospel witness through multiple forms of preaching.[1]

In this Appendix we illustrate how the two authors attempted to listen to the advice from the laity articulated in the previous twelve chapters while preparing two sermons. Each author reports the context of the sermon, provides the biblical text and summarizes the exegesis on which the sermon is based. In a sermon on a passage from the First Testament, Ron Allen precedes his sermon with an extended discussion of how he tried to draw on advice from the laity reported in the earlier part of the book. In a sermon from the Second Testament, Mary Alice Mulligan uses the mode of running commentary at the bottoms of pages to do the same. Although the biblical texts are different, they deal with similar themes—foolishness and wisdom, faithfulness, living in covenant with God and others, and the role of material resources in community. The sermons make some similar points (though designed for the different contexts for which they were prepared). However, the sermons are also quite different, thus illustrating diverse ways of preaching in view of the twelve pieces of advice imparted by the listeners in the preceding twelve chapters.

"Fools Say in Their Hearts, 'There Is No God'"
A Sermon on Psalm 14 by Ron Allen

A minister-friend and spouse were expecting the birth of their second child, and I gladly agreed to be on call to preach in the event that the birth occurred late in the week. Normally, that preacher follows the lectionary. On Thursday night the child was born with the help of a midwife in the manse. When the phone call announcing the birth came, I was in the middle of preparing a sermon on a text that had been given to me for another event two weeks away. I did not have a message on the lectionary text in my "barrel," nor did I have time to prepare such a sermon. While I had other sermons in the barrel, my personal energy tends to be higher when preaching a fresh message, so I tried to adapt the sermon that was in process to the congregation for the next Sunday.

Although the congregation is a part of my own denomination, the Christian Church (Disciples of Christ), I had not previously visited there. I expected that the congregation—made up primarily of senior adults—would be excited about the birth in the pastoral family. I was aware that the community had been a major manufacturing center but had experienced the closing of several plants (and subsequent loss of jobs). The congregation is made up largely of middle-class and upper-middle-class business owners, management personnel, educators, and other professionals. Like other churches in the Christian Church (Disciples of Christ), the congregation observes, every Sunday, the Supper of Christ to which I, like many Disciples preachers, make reference at the close of the sermon.

Biblical Text: Psalm 14

Fools say in their hearts, "There is no God."
> They are corrupt, they do abominable deeds;
> there is no one who does good.
The LORD looks down from heaven on humankind
> to see if there are any who are wise,
> who seek after God.
They have all gone astray, they are all alike perverse;
> there is no one who does good,
> no, not one.
Have they no knowledge, all the evildoers
> who eat up my people as they eat bread,
> and do not call upon the LORD?
There they shall be in great terror,
> for God is with the company of the righteous.
You would confound the plans of the poor,
> but the LORD is their refuge.

O that deliverance for Israel would come from Zion!
When the LORD restores the fortunes of [the] people,
Jacob will rejoice; Israel will be glad.

The movement of the sermon follows the basic movement of my exegetical encounter with the text. I began my work with the passage with a preunderstanding, suggested by long-standing familiarity with the opening verse ("Fools say in their hearts, 'There is no God'"). That preunderstanding is that Psalm 14 deals with the issue of believing in the existence of God. However, I soon realized that I had never considered that verse from the perspective of antiquity, nor had I given any thought to the rest of the psalm in the literary and theological contexts of interpretation.

Psalm 14 combines prophetic and wisdom themes to speak to a congregation described variously as a "company of the righteous," the "poor," Israel in need of "deliverance," and a people whose fortunes are in need of "restoration" (Ps. 14:5–7).[2] The passage provides a lens for these people (who are faithful but socially disadvantaged and perhaps even exploited) to distinguish between the foolish and the wise. The psalm assures the community that God will restore their life and will hold fools accountable for the ways in which they have destroyed the covenantal quality of life that God seeks for all. The text encourages the community to remain wise and faithful so that they will avoid the fate of the foolish who fall under the judgment of God in a moment of "great terror" (14:5a), and will be a part of the congregation experiencing deliverance when God restores their fortunes (14:7). The text also warns the foolish to turn from their community-destroying ways and to "seek after God."

The commentaries point out that the opening observation, "Fools say in their heart, 'There is no God,'" does not refer to a theoretical discussion of the existence of God. Rather, it refers to the fact that fools live as if they are not accountable to God for violating God's purposes, which are for all to experience fullness of blessing in community (Ps. 14:1). The term "fool" (*nabal*) refers not to those who are not very smart, but as in the prophetic and wisdom traditions, to those who do not adequately live in response to God's aim for covenantal relationship with one another and with the earth. The wise, by contrast, understand and live consistently with the divine purposes.

The psalmist pictures God looking down from heaven to see if there are any who are "wise, who seek after God" (14:2). Before studying the text, I assumed that the latter phrase refers to intense experiences of prayer in which individuals and communities seek God's guidance. But the commentaries point out that this expression means seeking to live under God's rule, to live in supportive community according to God's covenantal design.[3] In hyperbole, the psalmist declares, "there is no one who does good" (14:3).

When the text asks, "Have they no knowledge?" the psalmist has in mind the knowledge of God's desires for human community. The evidence that the community does not possess such knowledge is that evildoers (in the most vivid expression in the psalm) "eat up my people as they eat bread" and "do not call upon the LORD" (i.e., do not repent and take up God's design for living).

This flagrant and widespread disregard for God's aims will lead to a time when the foolish are in "great terror" (14:5). The psalmist anticipates a moment when God will step into history and punish the evildoers. In a similar way, God will also deliver Israel and restore the fortunes of God's people (14:7). For God is "with the company of the righteous" (14:5) and is the "refuge" of the poor.

Most of the time, I use a hermeneutic of analogy to move from the purpose of a Bible passage in its ancient setting to its possible functions for today's congregation.[4] I could see two possible analogies arising from this text. Is the congregation in a situation more like that of the company of the righteous or more like that of the fools? If the former, the sermon would explore how the psalm assures the struggling congregation that God is with them as they suffer indignity and exploitation from the foolish. If the latter, the sermon would explore how the text could help the congregation recognize their complicity in foolishness and try to lure them toward a wiser life. I prepared the sermon based on the latter analogy because I had gathered in conversations with the minister that the congregation–like so many predominately Anglo congregations–is caught up in middle-class values associated with the consumer culture in North America.

Listening to the Advice from the Listeners

In the discussion that follows, I indicate how I tried to take the twelve perspectives articulated in this book into account in moving from the exegesis to a sermon for the congregational context described above. Although these perspectives are discussed separately, their concerns relate with one another. For purposes of discussion we separate the different perspectives, but in actual sermons they work together.

With respect to *making it plain* (chapter 7), I summarized in one sentence the major message of the sermon: God empowers the congregation to turn away from a foolish life and toward a wise one. I hoped that the congregation would turn away from ideas and behaviors that eat other people (with the consequence of being eaten themselves) to participate in attitudes and actions that feed the world so that all can live in the blessing that God intends. I state this point directly toward the end of the sermon (as annotated below).

The opening line of the text is reasonably familiar but often understood out of context, a misunderstanding I shared as I came to the text. Thus I decided to let the movement of the sermon follow the movement of my process of discovering what the text intended to do in its ancient context. I moved from misconception to understanding and application.

The *Bible* (chapter 4) is central to the sermon. I envisioned the sermon as conversational in character involving mutual critical correlation of the psalm, the congregation, contemporary North American culture, and me.[5] I sought to identify points at which the psalm correlated with (and criticized) the experience of the congregation in North American culture, and vice versa. I tried to *make the Bible come alive* by explaining the meanings of key notions in their ancient context (such as foolishness and wisdom) and by finding specific analogies from the world of today. I tried to stay close to the language and movement of the psalm. In the latter two-thirds of the sermon, the movement of the message follows the movement of the text itself: from the consequences of foolishness, to the implicit appeal to the congregation to live wisely.

The purpose of the conversation is to *help the congregation figure out what God wants* (chapter 1), that is, to offer a theological interpretation. As the conversation developed, I recognized the wisdom of the critics who call attention to the fact that many aspects of North Americana are exploitative, unjust, and violent. In the language of the psalm, such attitudes and behaviors reveal that powerful persons and forces in North America live as if "there is no God." To continue the language of the psalm, they are foolish, corrupt, astray, perverse, and evildoers. I wanted the sermon to help the congregation name such phenomena and recognize how distant they are from God's purposes. I also wanted the congregation to recognize that, from the point of view of the psalm, such thoughts and actions have destructive consequences for community.

The task of figuring out what God wants overlaps with discovering *how the sermon helps the community* (chapter 5). The desire on the part of the interviewees to know "how the gospel helps us" is consistent with one of my fundamental convictions: Most sermons need to contain a word of good news, that is, an interpretation of how God is present and acting for the good of the community. The psalm itself suggests that God is with the company of the righteous, is a refuge for the poor (those who suffer exploitation), and will deliver the community and restore its fortunes. In this spirit I decided to use the psalm as a pastoral warning and to invite the congregation to recognize points at which God is at work to help the world become less a sphere of foolishness (anti-community) and more a sphere of wisdom (covenantal community).

A part of *showing how the gospel helps us* (chapter 5) relates to *talking about anything and everything* (chapter 8) as well as *helping the congregation get it right* (chapter 10). A part of the congregation's wanting to *get it right* is their willingness to recognize points at which they are complicit in thoughts and actions that, in the language of the text, are foolish. The sermon needed to help the congregation identify such situations. Given the fact that people are willing for the preacher to discuss "anything and everything," I felt the freedom to apply the major insight to any arena of life, so long as I did so respectfully. I tried to identify examples that relate to individuals, the congregation, and the broader culture. I also tried to pick examples that were current and with which the congregation could identify. The statewide news recently had a headline case of parents who were arrested for spending virtually all their money on drugs while neglecting their children. The town in which the congregation is located has suffered the loss of a major manufacturing industry, leaving many people unemployed or underemployed. Big corporations eat smaller ones.

I did not plan to include the example of getting a plastic cup at a fast-food restaurant and becoming aware of ecological wastefulness. That idea occurred to me when we stopped at a fast-food place as we drove from our home in Indianapolis to the town where the congregation was located. As noted in the reflection after the sermon, the waste of plastic from fast-food outlets is the one specific element of the sermon about which people commented afterward.

Another part of *helping the congregation get it right* (chapter 10) is encouraging the listeners to identify points at which they can take positive actions that are consistent with the gospel. In the words of the text, they want to learn how to live wisely. In addition to providing information about what it meant to be wise in the world of the Bible, the sermon suggests (in the last third) how people can respond to situations of folly. In the strength of God's empowering presence, the congregation can turn from folly to situations in which wisdom operates (parents on drugs seeking treatment, working with groups that seek a more just economic order, the preservation of the earth).

As a visiting preacher, I often think it is important to *speak from your own experience* (chapter 3) to help establish a human connection with the congregation, so long as the personal reference serves the purpose of the sermon and does not call attention to oneself. I made some remarks of a more personal nature prior to publicly reading Psalm 14, commenting on my warm and long relationship with the preacher and spouse and on the joy of the birth in the ministerial household. In the sermon itself, I referred directly to my own experience with respect to the movement of my interpretation of the psalm, from first impression to more mature determination, to a recent experience with one of our youth in the surf at sunset, and to eating.

The sermon provided a forum in which I could *be honest about what I really think* (chapter 9) regarding the relationship of typical North American values and practices, and their relationship with the gospel. I intended for the statement to be clear but respectful and to avoid caricature. At one point I was not fully forthcoming, though a sensitive listener could tell where I stand.

Since I was a first-time guest and unknown to the congregation, they had no perception of whether I *walk the walk* (chapter 2). While I was, in fact, honest about my theological convictions, the congregation did not know that for certain. The sermon did not unfold in such a way as to allow me to talk about my own modest commitments and actions with respect to foolish and wise behavior as defined in the psalm.

I intended to *keep it short* (chapter 6), especially since my observation is that congregations are often less attentive to visiting clergy than to their trustworthy local pastors. I did keep the sermon at the length to which the congregation is socialized (twenty minutes) but did not really keep it shorter than is usual for them.

I arrived early enough to work with the person who operated the public address system to learn how to use the microphone so that I would *talk loud enough to be heard* (chapter 11). As far as I know, this effort was successful.

The Sermon

(The italic annotations refer to material in the sermon that appears above the italics, except as noted.)

Something happened to me while I worked with the psalm. What happened happens so often when you work with the Bible. I look at the text, and, boom, I think I get its point and where the sermon is going.

"Fools say in their heart, 'There is no God.'" Atheists. A lot of families have one. Very hush-hush. "You know, Cousin Sydney doesn't believe in God," as if atheism is a contagious disease.

> *The sermon immediately reveals that the Bible is central and that the sermon will have a point. As I indicated in the comments above, the sermon begins with a sympathetic presentation of a common misunderstanding of the text.*

A couple of weeks ago, I was in California with one of our youth looking at colleges, and we visited a beach. I was standing up to my knees in the warm surf, the breeze was stirring, and the sun was setting. The whole sky came alive with color as the ball of fire settled below the horizon. How can you see something like that and not believe in God?

I haven't actually seen the baby born in the parsonage at 9:22 p.m. last Thursday night—seven pounds, two ounces. But we have had five babies in our house. How can you hold a new little person and not believe in God?

> *Although the worship leaders have previously acknowledged the birth in the pastoral family and I mentioned it myself prior to reading the psalm, I hope this reference will help the congregation identify with the sermon.*

Those ideas were building up steam to be a pretty good sermon. Trouble is, studying the text let the steam out of the pressure cooker.

When I got out the Bible dictionary and looked up the Hebrew word for "fool" here, *nabal,* I found out that being a fool is not just a matter of mind, but is more a way of life. Being a fool is not so much thinking there is no God as it is living each day as if you are not accountable to God or to the community that God intends. To be a fool is to live as if you can do whatever you want to whomever you want for whatever purpose you have in mind–like that kid when you were in school who tried to extort lunch money from other kids when the teacher wasn't watching.

Now, the psalm contains a scene that would make a great shot in a Barbara Walters interview. God looks down from heaven to see "if there are any who are wise, / who seek after God." Can you picture that on your screen? God–hands stretched apart on the railing on the balcony of heaven–looking down for those who are "wise, who seek after God."

The sermon seeks to provide clear background information about the text and to help "make the Bible come alive" by making the analogy to the kid who extorts money and describing the scene as a Barbara Walters interview both here and below.

After that discovery about "fool," I wasn't surprised to learn from the Bible dictionary that the "wise," those who "seek after God," are not just those who *think* there is a God or who are smart, or who earnestly pray, but are those who *live as if* God is right here in the room with them. They know they are accountable to God and to the *community* that God wants. They know they are to relate to other people in love, peace, and supportive relationships and make it possible for everyone in the community to have the things they need to experience life as blessing.

Now, if I were operating the camera for the interview, I would shift from the face of God to what God sees on the earth. "They have all gone astray, / they are all alike perverse; / there is no one who does good, / no, not one." This language is hyperbole, of course. Overstatement. But overstatements catch your attention and help you see things you might not otherwise see. And these statements–going astray, being perverse, and not doing good–all have to do with not living in supportive, abundant, peaceful *community* in the way that God wants.

"Have they no knowledge, all the evildoers, / who eat up my people as they eat bread...?" What an image–people devouring other people. Yet, it happens.

Sometimes, seeing people eating other people is so obvious and so reprehensible: parents who take money they should spend for children and use it to buy drugs.

Sometimes, we regret seeing people eating other people, but still we go along with it. A chain comes along and puts in a super center down the road from a local store. Before you know it, the locally owned store is out of business. Gone. And the people they employed? No job. No health care. Oh, some of the locals may get jobs at the super center; but Handy Hardware closes, and the community is less of a community. Many of you know what

I mean, as you watched a whole industry get eaten up and disappear from your town. Our habit is to shake our heads and say, "It's just one of those things. They've got to learn to deal with it." The bottom line for the accountant and the stockholder may be to make a profit. But from the perspective of the Bible, the real bottom line is seeking after God.

Sometimes, this eating up of people is so subtle we hardly notice. On our way here this morning, we stopped at a fast-food restaurant, and they gave us our food in plastic containers. All these plastic containers we use. Oil sits in the earth for ten millennia and then in one day is turned into a plastic cup. The useful life of that cup from the time it is filled at the soda fountain until we throw it away is maybe ten minutes–ten millennia in the earth for ten minutes of convenience in a throwaway culture. We send it to the trash heap where it will exist as trash for another ten millennia.

It even happens in the church. Some congregations are known as "priest eaters." And occasionally ministers feed on parishioners to satisfy the ministers' egos.

These illustrations, drawn from "anything and everything," are designed to help the congregation recognize circumstances around which the congregation needs to "get it right." At this point, the sermon raises issues and prompts the community to think about problems.

"Have [such people] no knowledge?" Do they think there is no God? Do they think they can get away with it? Do they think they will never be called to account? Other passages in the Bible remind us that the eye of God is everywhere.[6] God neither slumbers nor sleeps. God is everywhere, all the time. Watching.[7]

Then the text comes to a chilling climax. "There [the fools] shall be in great terror." Fools may live as if there is no God, but there comes a day when fools–they and we–must face the consequences of what we do. "They shall be in great terror."

Elsewhere scripture teaches that those who kill with the sword are killed by the sword.[8] Those who live by eating others will eventually be eaten.

This emphasis on judgment and reckoning may make the psalm seem harsh. Even frightening. But if you hold the camera at the right angle, you see something more.

In this last third of the sermon, the attempt is to show "how the gospel helps us" by naming ways in which the psalm can lead the congregation to recognize and respond to God's love for them and for the world. This part of the sermon names what the preacher believes God wants for the community.

I see the psalm as pastoral warning. You might walk out the door of the church after the service and see a child in the parking lot bending over to pick up a terrapin. At the same time you may see a car about to swing around the corner and hit the child! What are you going to do? Every person here would do everything they could to save that child.

That is what is happening through the psalm: God calls out a warning to prevent you and me and this congregation and our world from the consequences of choices that destroy the community that God wants for all and that will eventually destroy us.

Under the brightness of this light, I confess to you that I do not preach this kind of warning much. My sermons are big on love and grace and peace. But here it is in the Bible. And if I care about God, people, and the world, I need to eat a good breakfast for strength, take a deep breath for courage, and sound a pastoral warning.

Another positive focus comes into view when we hear the text as an implicit invitation to turn from foolishness to wisdom. The wise are people who live as if there *is* a God. They live toward the community that God intends for all, to participate with God not in eating other people but in feeding them—both literally and figuratively.

> *I briefly try to make the point clearly by stating the main message of the sermon clearly and concisely. Here and in the following material, I intend to avoid works righteousness (leaving the impression that the congregation must engage in the ethical behaviors suggested in the sermon to receive God's love) by stressing God's omnipresence and gracious empowerment.*

An amazing thing: When you live as if there is a God, you discover God at every hand. "God is with the company of the righteous." "[God] is their refuge." "When [God] restores the fortunes of [the] people, Jacob will rejoice; Israel will be glad."

God is present. And when the Bible says that God is present, it means that God is at work in the world setting things right. We have the opportunity to participate with God and to experience God's empowering presence in the process.

A parent on drugs can find help in a recovery program, and God is there. A congregation can provide the kind of deeply satisfying experiences that people seek when they turn to drugs. By myself I may not be able to prevent a plant from closing, but I can work with Bread for the World in rethinking the world economy and discover that God is moving through that process. We don't have to eat at fast-food places. We can get up early enough to have breakfast at our own table before driving north.

> *The preacher hopes that the congregation will recognize that accepting the invitation of the psalm will prove to be good news from God. I also hope that these brief examples will spark the congregation to think of additional ways that they can "get it right," that is, put the good news of the sermon into practice.*

Now I know the psalmist does not have this in mind, but hearing about bread in a biblical passage almost genetically makes a Disciple think about the breaking of the loaf.

You sing the communion hymn. The elders pray over the loaf and the cup. The deacons move down from this beautiful table to pass the elements. You take the bread and feel its texture on your tongue. You drink the cup, and its sweetness fills your mouth. And an awesome feeling comes over you: God with you. Right here. In this very place at this very moment. With you, yes, and with all. Making us aware that we are all connected. Moving through us to live wisely, to live toward a world with bread enough for all.

"Fools say in their hearts, 'There is no God.'" In the presence of such love as we feel at this table, I want to be wise. What about you?

Reflection on the Sermon

Ministers who preach in the same congregation week after week often report that they get relatively little direct response from the congregation to specific sermons. Over time, of course, preachers can often see cumulative effects of their sermons in comments in meetings, in relationships in the congregation, and in the kinds of witness to which the people make commitments.

One of the hazards of being a guest preacher is that we seldom get meaningful feedback. That was the case in regard to the sermon just above. The congregation seemed attentive during the sermon. Only one person visibly fell asleep, and I was advised afterward that the person has done so every Sunday for many years. The church had an excellent public address system, and I think I brought the sermon to life in ways consistent with chapter 11 and its admonition to *talk loud enough so the congregation can hear.*

As anticipated, the community's energy was focused on the birth of the infant in the pastoral family. In retrospect, I think a sermon with a more celebrative tone would have better fit the occasion. In particular, the middle section of the sermon on people and groups eating others felt out of place. Taking a cue from the motif of showing us *how the gospel helps us,* I now think a sermon with a focus on giving thanks for and welcoming new life would have been more contextually appropriate.

The few people who commented on the sermon made customary remarks such as, "You stepped on my toes." One remark recurred in slightly different language from three different listeners. "I'll sure think about it the next time I get a soft drink in a plastic cup." Evidently, the image of the plastic cup made an impression on these listeners. They did not, however, indicate resolve to reduce their use of such materials, nor interest in searching for systemic ways to encourage North American society to become less of a culture of disposables.

"Being Rich toward God"
A Sermon on Luke 12:13–21 by Mary Alice Mulligan

This sermon was preached in a congregation in which, some years previously, I had served as interim pastor. Although appropriately away for about six years, I now worship with them occasionally. It was no surprise that during the current pastor's vacation, I was invited to fill the pulpit. We share a warm and friendly relationship, although no one is surprised when I speak pointedly from the pulpit about spiritual or social issues.

The congregation has a fairly solid sense of Christian mission and ministry, so a standard appeal from this passage in Luke to "share your surplus possessions" would not have blazed new ground for them. There are areas, however, where individuals are not able to cross barriers of difference, especially in matters of how the faith is lived out in life beyond the church walls. Some members of the congregation feel somewhat isolated because they hold minority (or perhaps merely less vocal) opinions on various matters of social ethics and personal behaviors. The elders of the congregation recently asked the congregation to consider systematically studying the role of gay men and lesbians in the life of faith. Although not yet ready for a full process of discernment, some congregants have nevertheless expressed hesitation, fearing that an eventual study could result in irreversible damage. Some believe an agenda has been set and any study will merely be a way for a pre-arranged decision to be imposed on the rest. The group conversation was due to start three weeks after this sermon was preached.

Recognizing that one sermon cannot do everything, I decided to follow the advice of this book. I limited the sermon to opening the parable to invite the congregation into a safe conversation about living out the faith together, although I also felt it useful to mention the specific topic of the elders' invitation, in order to model that such verbalizing is appropriate.

Biblical Text: Luke 12:13–21

> Someone in the crowd said to him, "Teacher, tell my brother to divide the family inheritance with me." But he said to him, "Friend, who set me to be a judge or arbitrator over you?" And he said to them, "Take care! Be on your guard against all kinds of greed; for one's life does not consist in the abundance of possessions." Then he told them a parable: "The land of a rich man produced abundantly. And he thought to himself, 'What should I do, for I have no place to store my crops?' Then he said, 'I will do this: I will pull down my barns and build larger ones, and there I will store all my grain and my goods. And I will say to my soul, 'Soul, you have ample goods laid up for many years; relax, eat, drink, be

merry.' But God said to him, 'You fool! This very night your life is being demanded of you. And the things you have prepared, whose will they be?' So it is with those who store up treasures for themselves but are not rich toward God."

This is a familiar passage for people who have been coming to church for a while. Often we hear sermons from it, questioning how we use our wealth or about becoming involved in greater mission work. As we study the passage, we need to keep in mind the importance of making the sermon fit the particular congregation and keeping the difficult balance between speaking the truth about controversial issues and making sure people do not feel beaten up by the ideas of the passage.

In his commentary on Luke, Fred Craddock sets the stage for this passage. Jesus is teaching his disciples while the crowd surrounds them. This situation allows anyone who wants it the opportunity to listen and follow. When someone calls out a request from the crowd, Jesus refuses to judge their inheritance quibble, for, in Craddock's words, "after all, who can judge whose greed is right?"[9] The voice from the crowd has asked Jesus to decide between two selfish alternatives.

Going right along with this idea, Richard Cassidy claims that Jesus tells the parable as an alternative to arbitrating between squabbling adult orphans. As such the parable helps us understand Jesus' stance on "surplus possessions." He explains: "It is important to recognize that the parable focuses upon the accumulation of additional goods by those who already have enough for their needs."[10] We hear the parable addressing what to do with the "more" once we have enough. But what else is going on?

Both Cassidy and Craddock point out that the farmer has not broken any laws. God's criticism is not that he has stolen from others or done evil. He is not an unjust sinner for building bigger barns for himself. He is a *fool*.[11] The word Eduard Schweizer uses to describe him is "stupid."[12] Something about keeping everything to oneself makes one a fool. We notice that in three sentences, the farmer uses the word "I" six times. He never makes a reference to any other person, not even as a conversation partner or for help in building the barn. He is wrapped up in his own world, which consists only of his own material goods. He is completely isolated.

The words Jesus speaks stand in stark contrast: "One's life does not consist in the abundance of possessions." The possessions have been the farmer's singular interest, but they "do not constitute life, and therefore he has not really lived."[13] The farmer has neglected to notice the needs or even the existence of humanity around him. By focusing only on himself, the farmer has neglected one of life's greatest possibilities. He could have become rich toward God.

But what does Luke mean by being "rich toward God"? It is partly an attitude about possessions, which disallows their grip on life. Recognizing this passage is leading up to Jesus' claim that "…where your treasure is, there your heart will be also" (12:34), we see more clearly that being rich toward God is about priorities of loyalty. A Bible dictionary, discussing "wealth," uses Luke 12 to point out that "Jesus was combating the insidious power of possessions to enslave [us] and destroy [our] ultimate trust in God and [the realm]."[14] For Luke, to be rich toward God necessitates using what material possessions we have for the mutual well-being of the community, with the confidence that in turn God will provide us with material blessings through the community. So the sermon may ask, how are we, in this congregation, to be rich toward God at this time?

The Sermon (a)

(Annotations at the bottoms of pages discuss how Mulligan incorporated in her sermon advice from listeners given earlier in this book.)

Here's the set-up for the upcoming passage. Jesus is presented as teaching his disciples and anyone else who wants to listen. From the back of the crowd, someone calls out to Jesus to settle a family inheritance dispute. Brothers are haggling over who gets what. Does the larger portion go to the older son or should the younger son receive an equal amount? Although, on many occasions, Jesus is happy to correct people's behavior or opinions, this time he refuses to take sides; and instead, he tells a parable.

One of the commentators on the passage, Disciples scholar Fred Craddock, explained that Jesus refuses to judge between these brothers because the real question the onlooker poses is, "Whose greed is right?" Whose *greed* is right? No wonder Jesus tells a parable to offer a totally different way to look at the issue. Jesus gives us a different perspective. Listen for the Word of God. (b)

(a) In order to communicate that the sermon will be grounded in scripture, the preacher begins by introducing the passage before reading it. Many preachers report that they find this practice quite useful for making the reading more understandable.

(b) We know from chapter 4 and various other places in this book that most people want the sermon to be based on the Bible. In addition they want the sermon to open the Bible's meaning and make it come alive in this congregation. Using an exegetical introduction before reading the passage allows the congregation to know the sermon will be biblically based, coming from a particular passage. However, the preacher also notes the teaching from a commentary, written by a scholar from their denomination. The initial exegesis before reading the passage aloud assists the congregation's comprehension of what the passage is about and begins unpacking the ideas it presents. The explanation before reading the Bible also introduces an idea (although in a subtle way) that will run through the sermon, namely that we need to break out of our either-or thinking to discover the richness of diverse ideas among us. Jesus offers a different perspective from the false choices presented by the inheritance dispute. For those who have told us they want some flexibility in the service, introducing the scripture before reading it may be interesting.

[*Here read the passage:* Luke 12:13–21]

You know self-centered individuals. You've seen people who are only concerned about themselves. *Numero Uno* is the single focus for some folks, as if "one" is the only number they ever learned. And haven't you heard the joke of the person who says, "I've been going on and on about myself. So now it's your turn. What do you think about me?" Really, aren't there individuals who are just so full of themselves? The only song they seem to know is not "We Are the World," but "I Am the World." It's all about me, me, and of course, me. (c)

These individuals seem wrapped up in accumulating more and more and more, all for themselves. Athletes are reported as "collecting" luxury vehicles. Remember reading some months back that one basketball star has *six*? TV stars have their own "*collectibles*." How many houses does one person need? But not just celebrities. You know them, people who seem to wake up every morning saying, "What do I want to buy myself today? a new boat? furs? redecorate the living room? Something smaller? maybe diamonds?" You see them in stores, arms full of packages; and you suspect inside each box is something they bought for themselves. New shoes? clothes? new china? a few more knick knacks? some more stuffed animals that they will have to stuff onto their already over-stuffed shelves at home? (d)

The man in Jesus' parable was not the wealthiest landowner in the area; he had probably just had a few exceptionally good years. His old barns were no longer big enough. But, the problem wasn't his successful harvest. The problem was his self-centered isolation. When he was stumped by his abundance, notice: He had no one to talk it over with but himself. Listen! Jesus reports: "He thought to himself, 'What should I do, for I have no place to store my crops?'"

Well, you remember the story. "I will pull down...I will store all my grain...And I will say to my soul..." What a sad character.(e) He probably

---

(c) The sermon opens recalling experiences with folks who are all wrapped up in themselves. Several people in our research indicated that a little humor helps keep attention, so some lightness is inserted. Humor can also relax people, disarming their defenses, which is useful when sensitive issues are about to be raised. Also, using the caricature of the selfish person allows listeners to want to identify themselves as belonging to another category.

(d) Here is just a hint that congregants might be included in the selfish category. Listeners are aware that, although a guest to their pulpit, the preacher knows them quite well, even that some of them do collect stuffed animals (by the dozens). It is just a quick shadow of stepping on toes before moving to exegesis.

(e) Here we try to understand what the person in the biblical passage is about. As noted in several chapters, people interviewed want to hear the Bible explained from the pulpit. The parable seems easy enough, but listeners are eager to have their understandings confirmed or corrected. In an effort to keep the sermon short and focused, exegesis is limited to what is directly relevant for the meaning of this sermon.

had one of those T-shirts with the saying, "The one who dies with the most toys, wins." *Wins?* Wins what? Can't you see him? All wrapped up in himself, gathering more and more stuff. And then he dies. And there's all that stuff. Tons of stuff. How sad. Jesus is clear, however. The behavior of the wealthy landowner does not make him a sinner, just a fool. The rich farmer is a self-centered *fool,* with only himself to care about, or talk to, or do things for. You know selfish people just like him. (f)

But we are to be rich toward God. Christians are to have their wealth in God. What a profound-sounding phrase: "Rich toward God." But like many religious phrases, we really need to stop and figure it out. What does it mean for us to be rich toward God? (g) From study of the setting of the

---

(f) In superimposing a T-shirt on our ancient character, we not only see him among us, we recognize that selfish isolation crosses millennia. The description opens the Bible and then makes it live in modern garb. If the farmer can be like us (wearing a shirt that reveals who he is), then we must admit we can be like him (lost in our own possessions). If we can be like him, we also need to feel the emptiness of having only "stuff" after our lives pass. Leaving "stuff" hanging in the sermonic air allows the hearers to feel the futility of accumulating more than they need. To communicate as fully as the interviewees advise us, the sermon tries to help people sense the meaning intellectually and emotionally. We want them to comprehend the futility of having abundance beyond one's needs, at the same time they feel the emptiness of all that stuff when life is passing. A slight clip in the delivery of the short sentences, along with some pauses between them, should help embody the meaning. The voice could be more pointed here, since these folks are used to sermons talking about possessions.

(g) Although it is easy for most laity to identify selfish people, the more important piece is for them to understand the right way to be, so here we make the important shift. We turn from looking at the inadequacy of the isolated life to see what an appropriate alternative is. Our lay listeners have been very clear that they want sermons that make sense of religious ideas. It is not helpful merely to say we must be rich toward God, as if that were somehow a self-explanatory direction. "Go be rich toward God, and you will live a happy life." Our interviewees were clear; the preacher needs to help the congregation know what this religious language means. Also, by stopping the flow of the sermon briefly to ask what does this mean, the preacher is revealing a little of her own humanity. Instead of acting like everyone should know what such phrases mean, the preacher is showing an understanding of the congregation, composed of lots of people who may not have a clue what "being rich toward God" means. Also, the pause to admit our need to figure out this religious language serves to slide the preacher's humanity right into the pew with the rest of the congregation. As the laity have requested, the minister is revealing how her own faith growth parallels the laity's. Of course, we all have to think through what such phrases mean. In the next lines, the preacher demonstrates the technique of going back to what we do know from the passage. Thus, the sermon not only is serving to explain this idea, it is also modeling some biblical study tools. Remember, in the introduction to the scripture reading, I referred to a commentary. Such a reference also models how to investigate meanings.

parable, we know Jesus is talking about greed and self-centered isolation. So we get some clues about what being rich must not mean. Being rich toward God is not about how many hours a day each of us spends in our prayer closets conversing with Jesus. As important as private devotions are, they do not make us rich toward God. Being rich toward God is not being satisfied with our individual relationship with Jesus. Being rich toward God involves others. (h) When we are rich toward God, God has first dibs on all our energy, our possessions, and our attention; and God is directing us out of our absorption with self. To be rich toward God involves rejecting those practices that allow others to be deprived of what they need. Instead, we are to put our wealth into God's hands to be used for the welfare of the world. To be rich toward God means we pledge our possessions to the community's well-being, even as we live with a confidence that the resources of the community of faith will, in turn, provide us with material blessings.

To make sure we understand as fully as we can, let's ask someone who knows what being rich toward God means. An 85–year-old woman recently visited a wealthy friend, who lamented how unfair it was that her much less well-to-do friend had never had the kind of luxury she had enjoyed her whole adult life. The 85–year-old surprised her wealthy friend, saying, "We've never had much money, but we've always been rich! My husband and I always had everything we ever needed, and most everything we ever wanted."

At 85, this woman understands the meaning of being rich toward God. For her, it is a daily contentment with the blessings of family, a home (although they never *owned* one), good friends, and meaningful work. She knows the indescribable wealth of believing all life matters to God, which means God cares for her—every minute of every day, no matter what. And so she spends her life responding to others as she believes God wishes her to. Whenever she finds herself with more than she needs, she spreads the excess around; for she is more than satisfied with having *enough*. To hear

---

(h) As difficult as it is for some people to hear (and thus for some preachers to say), our lay listeners have told us that it is important to step on their toes when it means they will grow from it. Many people of faith find strength and meaning in daily private devotions, however this parable warns against isolation, which can be understood to include even the prayer closet. Of course, the preacher needs to note the value of personal devotion time, yet explain it is not what this parable is pointing us toward. Several places in previous chapters we note people's insistence on the importance of continuing assistance to grow in the faith. They want to know more, and they want to see how that knowledge can be played out in their lives. This part of the sermon is not rejecting private devotions, rather teaching what more the faith can be.

her talk, she clearly has a richer life than her financially wealthy friend. Her life is rich toward God. (i)

Some years ago, the youth group in this congregation experienced such a richness when we participated in a mission trip to Mexico. One of our projects was painting a woman's new house (such as it was), which another youth group had helped construct. Remember? A tiny little shack of a house, but it was hers; and she got to pick the color of exterior paint. Some of us remember, she chose bright pink. Eric, Josh, Anu, Chris, Alex, Ayinde, Valeria, Ren, Kimberly, Donna, Paula, and Don, up to their eyelashes in pink paint, and having a ball. They were not goofing around; they were seriously painting, but feeling a deep joy, because when we are doing God's work, we can feel the richness flowing among us. (j)

When we are rich toward God we live each day in gratitude; we experience divine joy and contentment in the well-being of those around us. Every day, when we recognize the blessing of God's companionship

---

(i) This vignette illustrates that elusive trait of being rich toward God. It also shows the minister is in touch with the people, if they reason the 85–year-old is a member. It may be easier to believe an 85–year-old could feel rich toward God in this way, after all she probably grew up in the Depression, yet the listeners should feel with her the contentment of having enough. Of course, preachers who serve congregations where members often do not have enough would need to be particularly sensitive about making claims of God's providence. The congregation where this sermon was preached is a predominantly blue-collar group. Some members experienced periods on welfare or unemployment, although most live comfortably. The preacher was aware that a good number had felt hard times, but the richness of having enough was something they all knew as well. Also, the preacher felt confident that this group would be able to agree that material wealth (although most had not experienced it) was not the most important way to be rich. Such insights show the listeners that the preacher is addressing this congregation personally.

(j) The illustrations attempt not just to show the idea, but also to facilitate the listeners' experiencing the joy and feeling rich toward God. Reminding people of a time they had experienced the richness is especially valuable. Not just an individual 85–year-old feels the richness. The youth group illustration reminds the listeners of a time many of them felt it, too. Even those who did not participate in this particular mission trip might remember similar experiences, or at least remember the richness reported when the youth returned home. Not only is it a good illustration, it again shows that the preacher is in touch with the congregation and knows their faith. In addition, it subtly reminds the congregation that the guest minister accompanied the youth on that particular mission trip, thus indicating the preacher's ability to walk the walk, and perhaps most importantly, to walk it with them. The illustration shows the preacher is one of them. It allows the minister to share herself with the congregation without resorting to using a personal story, which might be heard as self-focusing. A personal story would directly work against the ideas of this particular sermon that advise against self-centeredness and isolation.

along our earthly journey, what we are doing takes on holy significance. Others may be completely baffled that we do not judge our wealth according to the number or monetary value of personal possessions, but *our* wealth stems from something different. We are to be rich toward God. (k)

But to be rich, we need community. Our richness comes in the gift of the congregation. Only when we embrace the faith community do we become rich together. What we learn from all this is that we need each other if we are going to get the faith right. We don't become rich toward God alone. We become rich toward God together.

Now, none of us is so naïve as to think that there is always agreement in the faith community. (l) In fact, we can get so angry at each other we want to quit the church. Sometimes it just feels easier to stay away from any congregational gatherings, easier to stay home, read our Bibles to ourselves, locked away in private prayer, because when we are alone in our faith, we always feel we have gotten it right. Whereas in the church, surrounded by all these different people, we fight. We have serious disagreements over serious issues. People come to church to find answers to matters of life and death, so when we disagree, these are not casual topics. The differences of opinion and the arguments can threaten to tear us apart. Sometimes, it even feels as if we are individually getting torn apart, as if our hearts are being ripped from our chests. (m) Community

---

(k) The preacher has been careful to end this part of the sermon on a very positive note and to show that she is right with them. As a congregation, they are together; and they have experienced divine richness.

(l) If the sermon is going to turn to more difficult ideas, it is important that the preacher stays honest. No one will believe later statements about what a congregation may be unless the preacher has shared how difficult it can be to try to live the faith together. Again, the preacher's honesty shows knowledge of the community and the frustration many have felt. If the preacher is going to talk about anything and everything, honesty about what one really thinks is an essential precursor.

(m) The preacher is walking a thin line here, reminding those who have confided their hesitance and fear that they have been heard, yet not wanting them to feel their confidences have been betrayed. People know she has served in a pastoral capacity in the past. Thus, the preacher keeps the images vague enough that anyone may identify with the notion that communities can be painfully diverse bodies. We remember that our lay respondents have directed us not to oversimplify complex issues, so the pain and differences of opinion in the complex issues of community life and individual faith need to be admitted. There are two forces at work: keeping a focus specific enough to mean something to this group and, on the other hand, allowing the complexity of these real issues to come through. The sermon attempts an honest look at the reality of communal faith, while limiting the focus to the current scripture and the one topic that the elders have invited the congregation to consider, which has not even been mentioned so far.

can be very tough going. But we need each other. In fact, our differences are not only inevitable; they can enrich us. We need our different opinions. (n)

Think of the time when what must have been a 13' 2" truck was passing under a 13' 1" underpass, until the driver heard the truck scrape. He slowed down, but kept on pulling through; confident the truck could squeeze through–until the truck jammed tight. When the driver climbed out to survey the situation, he immediately saw a solution–a part of the overpass would have to be drilled away. As the crowd gathered, another side formed–the top of the truck would have to be sliced off. An argument followed. Each side was as firmly wedged in their opinion, as the truck beneath the underpass, until the little girl wondered aloud, "Why not just let some air out of the tires?" Letting air out could drop the truck roof at least an inch. And slowly the truck driver could steer the rig out. (o)

Sometimes we get so firm in whatever sides we've taken, we need others around us to show us *all* the options. We need each other. Without each other, we are less, and our solutions are limited. In her book about language in worship, liturgical scholar Gail Ramshaw writes that congregations need both the influences of the history and traditions of the faith, *and* the language of the modern world to make worship meaningful. "Christian speech is vernacular with a twist: the language of faith is a dialogue between our contemporary experience in its vernacular dress and the gospel written in the scriptures and repeated in the tradition." (p) She holds a commitment to the most powerful worship liturgies, prayers, and communion services, which are "both shaped by centuries of Christian tradition and informed by today's speech." (q) Our worship is enriched by using ancient language, with words so lush and powerful they almost stop our breath, but yet modified by the flow and comfort of contemporary

---

(n) This section has been difficult and ends with a claim many people may not be ready to accept.

(o) Again a touch of humor allows a break in the tension. Being church together is difficult, but people of faith need each other. The illustration moves the listeners quite far from the church building. No one really cares about the two sides of the argument in the story, yet the little girl's suggestion shows how a solution can come from within the group, yet not be from the two major positions. It is a safe illustration that does not point toward anyone in the pews. However, the discussion following the illustration brings it home.

(p) Gail Ramshaw, *Reviving Sacred Speech: The Meaning of Liturgical Language* (Akron, Ohio: OSL Publications, 2000), 4.

(q) Ibid., ix.

language usages. We need both history and the contemporary world if we are to worship God fully; after all God deserves the best we have to offer. (r)

Just as in our life together as a congregation, we are enriched by each other. When diverse members of the faith community surround us, we are best able to pay attention to the Spirit's leading us in the faith. We become rich toward God together. (s)

So we get to celebrate our community. Community is a gift from God. (t) So what about our congregation? Can we celebrate the richness of each other? Look around. No two people are alike. God has carefully created each person as a unique individual, according to a divine and loving plan. And for each of us, the circumstances of our lives continue to pound us into people even more diverse. The elders of the congregation have agreed that in our broad diversity, yet as a single congregation, now might be an appropriate time to study and discuss together issues of sexuality and the role of gay men and lesbians in our life of faith.

Such a study would be easier if we were all alike, all of the same opinion; but Jesus didn't call all one kind of person. Not even the promise of the

---

(r) Here an example from the study of liturgy moves the congregation back into the church building, showing that the two ingredients of historical faith language and modern vernacular speech make the finest worship experiences. God deserves the best, which comes from combining the two options. This example also models the importance of studying books in addition to the Bible and its commentaries. One final job this example accomplishes is in laying some groundwork, that a helpful conversation is possible even if the ever-threatening "worship war" raises its head a little higher here. The preacher knows of parking lot discussions about the lack of sophisticated theology in contemporary Christian songs versus the dry, dated, obscurity of classical Western European church music. Although this is not the day to talk about differences of opinion in liturgical components, to hint that peace is possible if the war comes is good foundational work.

(s) A word about sermon length: This congregation is used to eighteen- to twenty-minute sermons. If they were used to twelve minutes, the illustration about liturgical language could be cut, although it does several helpful things. If there were real rumblings about contemporary music or ancient language, the use of this material might not be fitting, since this group has enough on its plate with the approaching study. As our respondents directed us, we want to make the point plainly and keep the congregation focused in ways that will help them, without making them sit longer than they expect or including tangential material. Because this group was used to longer sermons and because the material reminds them that their diversity enriches their faith, the preacher left it in.

(t) Although the sermon has mentioned God a few times, it is only here we begin to get a sense of what God is doing. We know from the lay respondents that people want to hear more about God and where God might be leading them. So from here the sermon begins to help them figure out more specifically what God might want from them at this time.

afterlife was limited to one type of faithful follower. About the last person Jesus spoke to before he died was the thief on the next cross, whom he promised to meet in Paradise. (u) So believers have been a diverse group from the beginning, not by accident, but by God's plan. Our different opinions, as difficult as they are even to listen to sometimes, can serve to make us a more faithful church. We benefit from listening to each other and sharing the differences. (v)

Every congregation has a mixture of humanity. Some people like things more traditional, some lean toward the modern; some use sophisticated expressions, others blurt out whatever new idea enters their heads, others are quite methodical thinkers; some are willing to try anything, others cling to the old ways, which "don't need to be fixed if they ain't broke."

We might think of each person as providing an individual ingredient in a huge mixing bowl. Some folks add serious substance to the conversation, others remind us of the importance of not taking ourselves too seriously; some sort of lubricate our ability to talk about issues, others harken us back to our most solid foundations. Each adds something crucial to the process. When we get tossed into the bowl together and whipped around together, it frequently does not feel very good. But when all of our God-given strengths are mixed together in the presence of the heat of the Holy Spirit, we become something wonderful together.

All of our differences, baked in the heat of the Holy Spirit. Yum! Maybe we could think of the congregation as becoming cake together. More than any of our individual gifts, we become a gift to each other by the power of the Holy Spirit. We get to be cake! The community of faith is a tremendous gift. We get to revel in being together. We get to celebrate being the faith community.

What a richness! Instead of drowning in empty possessions that we can't even take with us, we get to be rich, fabulously wealthy toward God,

---

(u) In an effort not to confuse the congregation with what some of our interviewees refer to as "flipping" all over the Bible, the preacher alludes to the story of the thief on the cross, found in Luke 23 (thus keeping in the same gospel); but does not have people turn to it. Referring to the story in this way serves to teach the one detail to those who did not know it, without diverting attention away from the flow of the sermon ideas.

(v) This crucial claim of divine intention to our diversity in the midst of acknowledging our preference for unanimity is the key for the complex claims made in this sermon. The church needs its disagreements to be what God wants us to be. The answers come not from silencing the minority voices, but by listening to all, thinking together, and waiting for new possibilities to be discovered among the members. However, as our listeners reported, congregants want to be invited into the thinking process, not just have answers or opinions handed to them. They want their priests and ministers to help provide the tools and join with the congregation in discovering the solutions.

now, by immersing ourselves in the sometimes sticky, but always necessary, community of Jesus. Only when all of us are together, we get to be cake!

Reflection on the Sermon

There is a congregational culture here that allows stirring around during the sermon. People whisper, put on lotion, goo-goo at babies, take restroom breaks, and find chewing gum in their purses; so when preaching I try not to notice their behavior much. However, they seemed quieter and more focused on this day. That may just be wishful thinking, since I so wanted the sermon to encourage them toward their conversation.

Following the sermon, the lay leader who gave the invitation to the offering told how sharing increases what we have (a fitting Lukan idea). The invitation to communion played with the image of bread as a sign of our being cake. So at least those two persons heard the sermon with appreciation.

After worship, the first comment at the door, from one of those opposed to full inclusion of gay men and lesbians, was very positive. Many others also responded thoughtfully and with appreciation, although this is the common reaction I receive when I preach there. The most outspoken opponent to the conversation thanked me for "being our pastor, today." He did not speak of the sermon. I do not know if he was expressing appreciation for the pastoral way I dealt with the issue or merely using words that avoided thanking me for preaching.

Conclusions

The preceding sermons give a practical demonstration of how two preachers tried to heed the lessons from listeners interviewed for this study. Of course, preachers reading this book cannot simply lift either the sermons or the twelve principles articulated in the previous twelve chapters for use in their congregations, for sensitive pastors know the distinctive culture of values, feelings, preferences, and dislikes that make up their listening congregation. While ministers can profit from pondering the twelve pieces of advice in this study, the next step is for ministers to explore the traits of quality preaching and listening that are particular to their own congregations, and to shape sermons accordingly. The members of the project team have consistently found listeners to be among our best teachers. We believe local preachers will find that too.

Notes

Preface

[1]The four volumes published by Chalice Press work together as an informal series called "Channels of Listening" and are identified as such by the presence of a common logo on each volume.

[2]Our culture struggles to find adequate language for people with respect to racial ethnicity and culture. In this book, we typically speak of African Americans and Anglos (or persons of non-Hispanic European origin). The latter two terms are among those that are increasingly replacing the use of the word *white*.

[3]The project team comprised Ronald Allen (Director) of Christian Theological Seminary, Dale P. Andrews now of Boston University School of Theology, Jon L. Berquist of Westminster John Knox Press, L. Susan Bond of Brite Divinity School, John S. McClure of Vanderbilt Divinity School, Dan P. Moseley of Christian Theological Seminary, Mary Alice Mulligan (Associate Director) of Christian Theological Seminary, G. Lee Ramsey Jr. of Memphis Theological Seminary, Diane Turner-Sharazz of Methodist Theological School of Ohio, and Dawn Ottoni Wilhelm of Bethany Theological Seminary. Interviewers, in addition to several members of the project team, included Bobbye Brown, Lori Krause-Cayton, Owen Cayton, Lisa Coffman, and Edgar A. Towne. Congregations in the study were located largely in the Midwestern part of the United States and came from the following denominations and movements: African Methodist Episcopal Church, African Methodist Episcopal Zion Church, American Baptist Church, Christian Church (Disciples of Christ), Christian Churches and Churches of Christ, Church of the Brethren, Episcopal Church, Evangelical Lutheran Church of America, Mennonite Church, National Baptist Church, nondenominational churches, Presbyterian Church in the U.S.A., and the United Methodist Church. The questions that were asked are available in John S. McClure, Ronald J. Allen, Dale P. Andrews, L. Susan Bond, Dan P. Moseley, and G. Lee Ramsey Jr., *Listening to Listeners: Homiletical Case Studies* (St. Louis: Chalice Press, 2004), 181–84. Ministers were also interviewed, and plans are underway to share discoveries from pastor interviews in subsequent publications. A particular focus on the categories of *ethos, logos, pathos,* and embodiment is found in *Listening to Listeners* and in Ronald Allen, *Hearing the Sermon: Relationship, Content, Feeling* (St. Louis: Chalice Press, 2004).

Introduction

[1]Interviewers promised anonymity to the people interviewed. Consequently, when quoting someone from the study sample, we have sometimes slightly emended the interviewee's remarks to remove all material that would identify the person or the congregation. In our introductory remarks to the quotations, we provide further identification (such as gender, ethnicity, age, or congregational setting) only when such information greatly enhances our capacity to understand an interviewee's comments.

[2]For an overview of recent moves by preachers and scholars of preaching to take account of how listeners themselves say they perceive sermons, see Ronald J. Allen, "The Turn Toward the Listener: A Selective Review of a Recent Trend in Preaching," *Encounter* 64 (2003): 167–96. One should also see Lora-Ellen McKinney, *The View from the Pew: What Preachers Can Learn from Church Members* (Valley Forge, Pa.: Judson Press, 2003) and Lori Carrell, *The Great American Sermon Survey* (Wheaton, Ill.: Mainstay Church Resources, 2000).

[3]See the literature cited in Joseph R. Jeter Jr. and Ronald J. Allen, *One Gospel, Many Ears: Preaching and Different Listeners in the Congregation* (St. Louis: Chalice Press, 2002).

[4]Mary Alice Mulligan, Diane Turner-Sharazz, Dawn Ottoni Wilhelm, and Ronald J. Allen, *Believing in Preaching: What Listeners Hear in Sermons* (St. Louis: Chalice Press, 2005) explores *diversity* within the congregation with respect to the categories reported in the preface.

[5]For a general discussion of various ways of studying the congregation, see Scott L. Thumma, "Methods for Congregational Study" in *Studying Congregations: A New Handbook,* ed. Nancy T. Ammerman, Jackson W. Carroll, Carl S. Dudley, and William McKinney (Nashville: Abingdon Press, 1998), 196–239.

[6]For examples of written survey instruments, see Allen, "The Turn Toward the Listener," 189–91.

[7]For approaches to interviewing small groups and individuals concerning preaching, see the methods proposed in John S. McClure, Ronald J. Allen, Dale P. Andrews, L. Susan Bond, Dan P. Moseley, and G. Lee Ramsey Jr., *Listening to Listeners: Homiletical Case Studies* (St. Louis: Chalice Press, 2004), 149–67.

Chapter 1: Help Us Figure Out What God Wants

[1]In case the reader wants to know, the project team—in light of specific research areas—constructed the questions. They were discussed and modified in a meeting of our full board of advisors (nine professors of preaching and an editor who is also a biblical scholar) and our consultant (a professor of sociology of religion). They were then tested in pilot interviews and modified again. However, for any weaknesses in the questions, the authors of this book (director and associate director of the project) take full responsibility. For the questions themselves, see page 147, note 3 of the Introduction.

Chapter 3: Speak from Your Own Experience

[1]Kenneth Burke, one of the most influential writers in communication studies, sees identification as a key element in a speaking event. See Kenneth Burke, *A Rhetoric of Motives* (Berkeley: University of California Press, 1950, 1969), 69.

[2]Aristotle, *The "Art" of Rhetoric*, trans. John Henry Freeze. Loeb Classical Library (Cambridge: Harvard University Press, 1932), 17 (1.2.5).

[3]Congregants report that many other qualities in preaching also move them, such as emotion in the embodiment of the sermon, a sense of passion about the content, stories of people the congregation knows and loves, and stories of people in times of tragedy; and some people are stirred by ideas.

Chapter 4: Make the Bible Come Aive

[1]See pages 45–53 and 63–71.

[2]For a fuller discussion of clusters of viewpoints on the Bible in the congregations in the study, see Mary Alice Mulligan, Diane Turner-Sharazz, Dawn Ottoni-Wilhelm, and Ronald J. Allen, *Believing in Preaching: What Listeners Hear in Sermons* (St. Louis: Chalice Press, 2005), 21–45.

Chapter 6: Keep It Short

[1]Homiletics is the branch of theology that studies preaching; the homiletics professor is the one who teaches ministerial students to preach.

[2]David Buttrick, *Homiletic: Moves and Structures* (Philadelphia: Fortress Press, 1987), 140.

[3]Ibid., 140f (italics in original text).

Chapter 8: Talk about Everything

[1]For preaching on controversial or challenging subjects, see Mary Alice Mulligan, Diane Turner-Sharazz, Dawn Ottoni Wilhelm, and Ronald J. Allen in *Believing in Preaching: What Listeners Hear in Sermons* (St. Louis: Chalice Press, 2005), 91–110.

Chapter 11: Talk Loud Enough So We Can Hear

[1]For theoreticians of preaching who stress that the event of preaching is an embodiment, see Richard F. Ward, *Speaking from the Heart: Preaching with Passion.* Abingdon Preacher's Library (Nashville: Abingdon Press, 1992); idem., *Speaking of the Holy: The Art of Communication in Preaching* (St. Louis: Chalice Press, 2001); Charles Bartow, *God's Human Speech: A Practical Theology of Proclamation* (Grand Rapids: Wm. B. Eerdmans, 1997).

[2]Very few people in the interviewed congregations gave a negative evaluation of the minister preaching from a place other than the pulpit. However, since we did not ask about

this phenomenon, we cannot assume that silence implies that a majority of interviewees agree that preaching outside the pulpit can be a good thing. We report here the responses of people for whom the sermon from a location other than the pulpit is a sufficiently positive experience that they initiated their own comments on it. We also report one response that reveals dislike of a type of sermon that brings the preacher from the pulpit.

Chapter 12: Don't Forget to Put in Your Teeth

[1]For structured approaches to becoming acquainted with the congregation, see Joseph R. Jeter Jr. and Ronald J. Allen, *One Gospel, Many Ears: Preaching and Different Listeners in the Congregation* (St. Louis: Chalice Press, 2002); James R. Neiman and Thomas G. Rodgers, *Preaching from Pew to Pew* (Minneapolis: Fortress Press, 2001); Thomas Edward Frank, *The Soul of the Congregation: An Invitation to Congregational Reflection* (Nashville: Abingdon Press, 2000); Stephen Farris, *Preaching that Matters: The Bible and Our Lives* (Louisville: Westminster John Knox Press, 1998); Nancy T. Ammerman, Jackson W. Carroll, Carl S. Dudley, and William McKinney, eds., *Studying Congregations: A New Handbook* (Nashville: Abingdon Press, 1998); Leonora Tubbs Tisdale, *Preaching as Local Theology and Folk Art*, Fortress Resources for Preaching (Minneapolis: Fortress Press, 1997).

[2]For an approach, see John S. McClure, *The Roundtable Pulpit: Where Leadership and Preaching Meet* (Nashville: Abingdon Press, 1995).

[3]The authors of this book express reservations about sermons in which the preacher takes on the persona of a biblical character on pages 41–42.

Appendix: Putting the Advice to Work

[1]For discussion and sample sermons of thirty-four different approaches to preaching, see Ronald J. Allen, ed., *Patterns of Preaching: A Sermon Sampler* (St. Louis: Chalice Press, 1998).

[2]I found the following helps especially useful (though they do not always agree with one another nor do I always follow them): Peter C. Craigie, *The Psalms 1–50*, Word Biblical Commentary, ed. Bruce M. Metzger, David L. Hubbard and Glenn W. Barker (Dallas: Word Books, 1983), vol. 19; James Luther Mays, *The Psalms*, Interpretation: A Bible Commentary for Preaching and Teaching (Louisville: John Knox Press, 1994); J. Clinton McCann, "The Book of Psalms," *The New Interpreters' Bible*, ed. Leander E. Keck (Nashville: Abingdon Press, 1996), vol. 4.

[3]Note, especially, Patrick D. Miller, *Interpreting the Psalms* (Philadelphia: Fortress Press, 1986), 94–96.

[4]On the hermeneutic of analogy, the classic work is Stephen Farris, *Preaching that Matters: The Bible and Our Lives* (Louisville: Westminster John Knox Press, 1998).

[5]On the notion of sermon as conversation, see Ronald J. Allen, *Interpreting the Gospel: An Introduction to Preaching* (St. Louis: Chalice Press, 1998); idem. "Preaching as Mutual Critical Correlation through Conversation," in *Purposes of Preaching*, ed. Jana Childers (St. Louis: Chalice Press, 2004), 1–22; O. Wesley Allen, *The Homiletic of All Believers: A Conversational Approach to Proclamation* (Louisville: Westminster John Knox Press, 2005).

[6]Psalm 94:9; Ezekiel 5:11.

[7]Psalm 121:3–4.

[8]Revelation 13:10.

[9]Fred B. Craddock, *Luke,* Interpretation, a Bible commentary for teaching and preaching (Louisville: John Knox Press, 1990), 163.

[10]Richard J. Cassidy, *Jesus, Politics, and Society: A Study of Luke's Gospel* (Maryknoll: Orbis Books, 1978, 1992), 25.

[11]Ironically both sermons, without design, speak of fools. See Ron Allen's discussion, 125.

[12]Eduard Schweizer, *The Good News According to Luke,* trans. David Green (Atlanta: John Knox Press, 1984), 207.

[13]Ibid., 208.

[14]F. W. Young, "Wealth," *The Interpreters' Dictionary of the Bible* (Nashville: Abingdon Press, 1962, 1985), 4:819.